Prophecy Before Vision

Learning to See and Alter the Future

Inverting the Global Wealth Inequality Pyramid

An Ideology Platform for the Twenty-First Century

Copyright © 2024 James Michael Matthew.

All rights reserved. No part of this book may be used or reproduced by any means, graphic, electronic, or mechanical, including photocopying, recording, taping or by any information storage retrieval system without the written permission of the author except in the case of brief quotations embodied in critical articles and reviews.

This book is a work of non-fiction. Unless otherwise noted, the author and the publisher make no explicit guarantees as to the accuracy of the information contained in this book and in some cases, names of people and places have been altered to protect their privacy.

Inktrail Press LLC books may be ordered through booksellers or by contacting:

Inktrail Press LLC
330 N Brand Blvd. Glendale, CA 91203, USA
www.inktrailpress.com
323-800-3263

Because of the dynamic nature of the Internet, any web addresses or links contained in this book may have changed since publication and may no longer be valid. The views expressed in this work are solely those of the author and do not necessarily reflect the views of the publisher, and the publisher hereby disclaims any responsibility for them.

Any people depicted in stock imagery provided by Getty Images are models, and such images are being used for illustrative purposes only.
Certain stock imagery © Getty Images.

Interior Image Credit: US Census Bureau

979-8-9907665-2-5 (Paperback)
979-8-9907665-3-2 (eBook)
979-8-9907665-6-3 (Hardback)

Library of Congress Control Number: 2021924133

Print information available on the last page.

BOOKS AND AWARDS BY JAMES MICHAEL MATTHEW

PROPHECY BEFORE VISION

- Author Shout 2023 Reader Ready Award
- American Writing Awards 2022
- New England Book Festival Award 2022
- New York Book Festival honorable mention 2022
- Full page feature in *Bookmad's* second quarter issue of 2023 and social media

REJECT SELF-SERVING POWER

- London Book Festival Award 2023
- The BREW Book Excellence Award 2023
- Indies Today Award 2022

BUILDING THE CLIMATE CHANGE BRIDGE

- Los Angeles Times Festival of Books 2023
- New York Book Festival 2023

DEFEATING THE NEW AXIS POWERS

- 2023 Pacific Book Winner Awards
- Full page feature in Bookmad's first quarter issue of 2024 and social media announcement

THE TWO $20 TRILLION OPPORTUNITIES

THE LEADERSHIP BROADCASTING COMPANY

BUILDING THE SELFLESS ECONOMY

- eBookFairs Book Awards August 05, 2024
- 2024 American Writing Awards Finalist
- 2025 Author Shout Reader Ready Awards: Top Pick Selection

BUILDING FJORDS IN THE GREAT DESERTS

- 2024 American Writing Awards Finalist
- Reader Ready Awards 2025: Recommended Read Winner

ARTICLES BY JAMES MICHAEL MATTHEW

- Building Fjords in Nevada and Salt Marshes in Utah Author James Michael Matthew
- Matthew Writes a Bold New Approach to Climate Change and Global Crises
  - Introducing contrarian evolution and contrarian economics in the groundbreaking books, Building the Selfless Economy and Building Fjords in the Great Deserts

To my wife Susan and my four daughters Amy, Jennifer, Lenore, and Danielle, for joining me in our family quest: *inverting the global wealth inequality pyramid.*

Special Dedication

This book, my first of many to come, and therefore incredibly special to me, is dedicated to my sister Kay and my son-in-law Bruno, who we lost in 2020—the year we thought would never end and that truly changed us all forever. They now help guide us on our mission through signs from the Hall of Souls.

CONTENTS

Chapter 1 - The Wealth Inequality Pyramid 1

Chapter 2 - The Three Pendulums of a Society 15

Chapter 3 - Events to Happen—Things to Come 35

Chapter 4 - Linked Problems and Solutions 47

Chapter 5 - What Now? What's Next? 59

Chapter 6 - Case Studies: Learning Prophecy 65

Chapter 7 - My Prophecies for the Twenty-First Century 83

Chapter 8 - Let's Play Prophecy Poker 87

Notes 91

References 95

Figures 97

Exhibit 103

Previews

Building Fjords in the Great Deserts – Second Edition 105

Manufacture Like Nature Manufactures 106

Building Fjords in the Great Deserts – Third Edition 107

Contrarian Evolution and Contrarian Economics 108

5 Million Drone Boats, Ships, and Submersibles 109

Preemptive Strike 110

The Next Great Generation 111

ACKNOWLEDGMENTS

I am deeply grateful to all of the many homeless men, women, and children I met and spoke with while writing this book. During our travels throughout Florida, Atlanta, Austin, Baltimore, Honolulu, Los Angeles, Minneapolis, San Francisco, Seattle, St. Louis, and Venice Beach, we asked each of you the same question: why are you homeless? Your insights were stunning and diverse but held a common theme. Out of respect for your current situation in life, I have decided to forever keep those conversations confidential. I promise to all of you that I will never stop helping you and your colleagues to move back into America's mainstream of society.

INTRODUCTION

During my forty years as a financial executive, I have watched CEOs, boards of directors, investors, and senior management teams across many industries and types of organizations struggle mightily with articulating a vision for their organizations. I have come to believe they struggle because they have no, what I call, *prophecies* to base their vision upon. I am so passionate about my concept of *prophecy before vision* that I named our company after my passion.

My second passion of equivalent concern is, like many people, I have become increasingly alarmed in regard to wealth inequality, both domestically and globally. My concern and passion to reverse global wealth inequality became so great I finally decided to recruit my wife and four daughters to join me in launching our family business—JM Prophecies Corporation and the Susan Kay Matthew Foundation, both with the same mission: *inverting the global wealth inequality pyramid.* We plan to spend the rest of our lives pursuing this mission and helping as many people as we can move up the wealth inequality pyramid.

Our company combines these two passions and ideologies as our corporate foundation to pursue our mission. This book combines these two passions into *an ideology platform for the twenty-first century.*

This book is the first of many I plan to author as we pursue this quest together. I hope you enjoy reading it as much as I enjoyed writing it. I welcome you to join our family quest and help change the world by inverting the global wealth inequality pyramid, step by step, over the rest of our lives.

****

James Michael Matthew is an award-winning author, financial executive, and industrialist. He is the founder and chairman of JM Prophecies Corporation. His company's mission is tackling the major challenges of our times and building the selfless economy as it works to *invert the global wealth inequality pyramid.*

Mr. Matthew graduated from the Johns Hopkins University with a master's in biotechnology enterprise and entrepreneurship, an MBA from Michigan State University, and a Bachelor of Arts in accounting and auditing from the University of Illinois-Springfield. Mr. Matthew has completed postgraduate studies in law and sustainability and the future of sustainable business at the Smith School of Enterprise and the Environment, the University of Oxford; and artificial intelligence: implications for business strategy at the MIT Sloan School of Management.

CHAPTER 1

THE WEALTH INEQUALITY PYRAMID

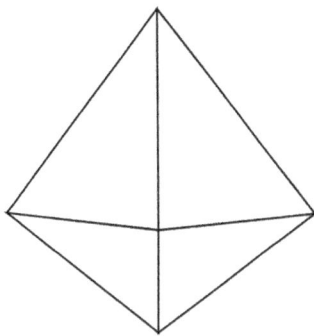

I begin the pursuit of *Prophecy before Vision: Learning to See and Altering the Future* with a discussion of global wealth inequality and JM Prophecies Corporation's quest to Building the Selfless Economy. I start my book with this topic because of its overwhelming significance regarding everything else. Almost everyone today understands and acknowledges that the global wealth inequality pyramid is not sustainable. Less acknowledged partners in wealth inequality are the large urban areas of the world that have become the serfdoms of our times. Although almost everyone agrees these inequalities are not sustainable, no one has any real answers to this global Armageddon. All approaches to resolving wealth inequality thus far fall basically into one of the following three camps: (1) taking money from wealthy persons and giving their confiscated (taxed) wealth to someone more needy; (2) relying on wealthy philanthropists to give their money away; or (3) just shrugging and ignoring wealth inequality because it has always existed. Neither of the first two approaches are sustainable because, eventually, the wealthy will run out of money to give away or confiscate. With these first two approaches, the wealthy also always run out of energy and time as the enormity of the inequalities sink in, washing away any progress they may have made. Camp 3 has run out of time and is approaching its end. We see and hear the proverbial canaries in the coal mine every day: mass domestic and global migration, homelessness and crime on unprecedented scales, and public frustration and hardening regarding what should be done.

Why do we at JM Prophecies Corporation believe we can be successful in reversing these long historical inequalities when so many others have failed over time and continue to flail about with no progress in sight? Conceptually, our approach is simple. Those who others see as drains on society, we see as our target markets. When others say you must get the "best" people in your organization to compete and succeed, we say no, we can actually build great businesses with "average" and "below-average" people who just want a chance at a better life (after all, the old cliché is true—ninety percent of life is just showing up). I am a devout capitalist and believe most of what Karl Marx wrote was rubbish. But Marx was right about one thing: that "true power lies in the masses, not for what they own but for what they can produce and consume over their lifetimes."

Although our plans are simple in concept, their implementation is by necessity complex. Such complexity is dictated by the enormity of the task before us. Our implementation strategies are summarized in our five steps to invert income and wealth inequality pyramids.

STEP 1:

DEVELOP AND PUBLISH NEW LEADERSHIP AND BUSINESS MODELS THAT PEOPLE CAN ADOPT TO IMPROVE THEIR PRODUCTIVITY AND INNOVATION, WHICH WILL REDUCE ALL LEVELS OF INEQUALITY

At JM Prophecies, we have adopted many conventional business principles, including innovation, which is at the core of our success. We have also created our own leadership principles and business models. Many of our models are discussed in this book, such as learning to predict the future and decision-making under uncertainty: making the right call one hundred percent of the time with only five to ten percent of the information. Four of our leadership principles are most relevant to our discussion here:

- **Prophecy before vision:** Forty years of observing and working with CEOs, boards of directors, and senior management teams have left me shaking my head in amazement at how mightily most struggle with succinctly articulating their vision for their organization. I am also amazed by how little research has been conducted on this topic. Over the years, I have often wondered how so many smart and highly educated people could struggle with the single most important aspect of their responsibilities. I have come to believe the reason people struggle so much with vision is they have no innate feel or understanding for what I call *prophecy*. Prophecy *must* come before vision. If you have no insight into what future external forces hold for your organization, how can you lead that organization? If you have no feel for what events are hurtling toward you and your company (e.g., global wealth inequality), how can you plan or prepare? I believe so passionately in this concept of prophecy before vision that I named our company accordingly. We begin with global demographics as the headwaters of our prophecies. We research global demographical data, and we prepare, monitor, and update our own global and domestic demographic forecasts.

- **Leadership means helping others be successful:** How many CEOs or boards of directors can honestly say their organizations believe in this principle and practice it religiously—or at all? Our mission keeps us from straying from this critically important principle. Whenever we are confronted with competing decisions, we simply ask ourselves: Which path will most help others be successful? The answer always leads us back to our true course.

- **Generosity is the new currency of our times:** In an ever-increasingly connected world, we have found that planting seeds of generosity reap nonstop harvests of future returns. As consumers grow weary of business models that target their pocketbooks, mindsharing and auctioning their personal data for no return, the companies that adopt generosity as the currency of our times will command customer loyalty that cannot be breached.

- **Target markets begin at the bottom of the inequality pyramid:** To be clear, our intent is *not* to be another do-gooder philanthropic organization. We have set out upon a great quest to invert the global wealth inequality pyramid both because we wish to change the world and because that is where the big opportunities are. Remember, Marx was right about one thing: "the power is in the masses." We buy real estate that nobody else wants. We embrace the neighborhoods with the absolute worst schools. We recruit the unemployed and, even better, the unemployable. We lend money to the so-called credit unworthy.

Why are we willing to take such risks, and how can we be successful when others cannot? Because we cherish and love doing what no one else will do. We assist and grow the intellectual base of the communities we invest in. A classic example we chuckle at is the conventional definition and construction of *low-income affordable housing*. Conventional wisdom means building multi-unit buildings and packing tenants into uncomfortable living quarters from day one. Inevitably, the investor ends up asking themselves years later, "What happened to my great property, and why is it now in such bad condition?" The answer to their question is they never even tried to change the intellectual fabric of the community or help the people in that community become successful. Conversely, we strengthen our members' intellectual fabric from the outset. We start with partnering with the local schools. We target the public schools struggling the most—those that are located across the line and have been for decades, right in plain sight, and have problems or barriers to their success that nobody can make a dent in, no matter how much taxpayer money is thrown at the problem. We establish our own underwriting standards that no competitor can even begin to comprehend, much less emulate. And finally, we define the value of a customer as the total incremental potential value of that customer—not by what they currently have but by what we can help them achieve.

STEP 2:

BUILD VALUABLE BUSINESSES DEMONSTRATING OUR NEW LEADERSHIP AND BUSINESS MODELS THAT ARE FOUNDED UNDER OUR WEALTH INEQUALITY REVERSAL MISSION

In order to maximize the returns on our new business model inventions, we launch and invest in our own businesses that adopt our new inventions. We focus on building entrepreneurs. We believe the serfdoms of our times are the result of millions of people leaving farms to go to big cities to find employment. This mass migration to large urban centers has destroyed much of the entrepreneurial spirit of our society. At JM Prophecies, we are about building that family farm/family business feeling and entrepreneurial spirit back into the population. Having grown up on a family farm in central Illinois, I know that feeling well and cherish my time there, growing up from a boy and into a man who had that opportunity to experience what family entrepreneurialism feels like and how it can help build an invincible society.

We target basic businesses that bottom pyramid members can understand and work with to build their lives. But more importantly, we also target cutting-edge 4.0-based companies and industries to move our bottom pyramid members up the pyramid value chain. Most current business school curriculums still advocate second industrial revolution business practices, but we believe in the fourth industrial revolution and are inventing new business models and economic theories for future public policy that will be more suited to third and fourth industrial revolution economies. We plan to publish additional economic theories and public policy recommendations in future publications.

We think globally but act locally. We think big but act and invest small. We purchase, locate, and position our commercial investments in the worst possible areas we can find—at the absolute bottom of the pyramid. These strategies allow our members to share in the wealth they help create.

When traditional investors say focus, focus, focus, we say diversify to the maximum extent possible in order to build a broad economic tent with enough revenue streams so members can enter and select which economic ladders best fit their interests and skills.

We think philanthropically, preferring to invest in companies that build top-line revenues to employ more members over businesses that focus on driving bottom-line net profits. But we act as private investors. One of our guiding philanthropic principles is *nothing happens until you build a business around it.*

We are contrarian investors and quick-to-act opportunists who exploit fissures in what we call the three pendulums of a society. The three pendulums are the subject of Chapter 2 and explain what we believe will set the tone for future economic and public policy in the US and beyond.

# STEP 3:

PROVIDE PLATFORMS FOR THOSE IN THE MIDDLE AND UPPER BOTTOM OF THE INEQUALITY PYRAMID TO HELP THEMSELVES ADVANCE UP THE PYRAMID.

A huge untapped market of potential future entrepreneurs exists in these segments of the US and global populations, just waiting and yearning to be mined for their potential. We vigorously believe in and plan to invest heavily in multiple types of incubators to identify our army of entrepreneurs. These incubators can be both virtual and physical in form. The most successful incubators must include investment funding for the resident entrepreneurs. We will invest in both majority- and minority-owned incubator companies. We also look to assist our investee companies in raising additional rounds of capital currently beyond our own financial capabilities.

# STEP 4:

PROVIDE PLATFORMS FOR THOSE IN THE BOTTOM OF THE INEQUALITY PYRAMIDS TO RECEIVE SHORT-TERM ASSISTANCE IN RETURN FOR LONG-TERM PAYBACK.

These target market segments comprise our single largest target market for residential real estate. Our strategy is to acquire bottom-of-market properties and build up the intellectual capacity of the residential population. We partner with community schools, churches, municipal governments, and other local community organizations to help build that intellectual fabric, including all age levels but primarily high school through adult education.

Unlike most real estate investors in pyramid-bottom communities who will build only multi-unit properties, we are not advocates of multi-unit properties. Instead, we invest in traditional single-family homes. This strategy helps build family units and increases the overall value of the communities and real estate properties in those communities.

We also are sensitive to avoid gentrification. We believe in creating a several multiple increase in valuation, but we also believe in the original owners participating in those valuations and building their own wealth.

By constantly looking to help our members at the bottom of the inequality pyramid, we are simultaneously increasing the wealth of those higher in the pyramid through better surrounding communities, more robust local economies, fewer taxes and public services required, and so on.

We segment the bottom and middle sections of the inequality pyramid into many granularly defined separate target markets. We focus on those target market segments that need our help and currently do not flourish on their own. We avoid complementary market segments that can be successful on their own. For example, we target aging-out foster care children but avoid high school seniors already college bound on their own. We target high school dropouts, pregnant young women with no partners, boys with no fathers, and homeless families. A picture of St. Jude, the saint of lost causes, hangs in my office to remind me and my colleagues who our target market segments are.

STEP 5:

REMOVE CRIME, ADDICTION, MENTAL ILLNESS, AND HOMELESSNESS FROM COMMUNITIES AND ASSIST THOSE POPULATIONS SEPARATELY.

Step 5 is the most difficult of our business model. Step 5 revolves around the belief and strategy that these target market segments (yes, these are target markets) have common causality and can therefore have common solutions. Our pilot products to approach these target segments include the following:

- **JM Prophecies Brain Care Corporation**: Our health care company dedicated to the study of brain health. Our initial targets include:
  - Developing a broad group of partnerships with health care providers, municipal organizations, and other not-for-profit organizations dedicated to serving these populations to develop common solutions.
  - Using these partnerships to accumulate a large database of brain scans to study for common causality and potential common solutions.
  - Development of a cell therapy company to conduct research for potential common solutions using brain cell therapy.
- **JM Prophecies Family Services—Code Red Product:** We all make mistakes in life. One of the keys to a successful life is: Don't make mistakes you *never* stop paying for—a life catastrophe moment. If you ask the majority of people in prison or who have been in prison, "How long did you think about the act that sent you to prison?" almost all respond with some version of "A second or

two—just a flash in time." Most crimes and other tragedies happen in a flash, a nanosecond of time in a person's life. And the victims, if included in the act, are forever changed for the worse, sometimes resulting in the loss of life itself.

We have yet to develop this catastrophic life moment product, but our plan is to offer a *code red* warning and prevention product through an online community-based family-services product. The concept is to immediately bring together a community to say, "No. Do not do that," and prevent those mistakes in life.

- **Drug-Free and Secure, Safe Haven Villages**: Safe places where addicts can heal and make new lives for themselves. Battling the ravages on our society due to drug addiction and crime is a main focus. Our current thinking is to construct a village of concentric circles or town squares with prisons at the innermost square, with expanding outer squares of security and patrols that can allow prisoners, addicts, homeless, and mental illness patients to someday resume normal outside lives but perhaps never actually leave the confines of a controlled environment. Our theory is that these concentric villagers could help one another. Remember, leadership is helping others be successful. Just because someone has stumbled in life and perhaps unfortunately made that mistake they will never stop paying for does not mean they cannot lead happy and productive lives helping others in the concentric village squares. Villagers' families and friends could also become villagers in outermost circles or squares in relatively free and unsecured areas, going outward but still subject to increasing levels of security and control as they travel inward.

- **Trauma Institute**: Most adverse behaviors begin with a traumatic experience. Trauma often comes from some form of abuse, often at an early age. Trauma can also begin with the sudden loss of a loved one through divorce, death, addiction of a family member, or one of many other traumatic experiences. We plan to establish a trauma institute with many partners and someday locate a physical trauma institute in our village squares.

- **Push-Pull Strategy Underlying JM Prophecies Brain Care**: JM Prophecies Brain Care will utilize a push-pull strategy whereby villagers under the justice system will be pushed into the villages under normal judicial practices and processes. Villagers not under the justice system will be pulled into the villages through their own decisions and pursuit of being close to family members, having access to a safe, drug-free environment, education, and employment within the villages' perimeter.

- **JM Prophecies Brain Care Public/Private Partnerships**: Existing prisons, jails, and other publicly owned and operated facilities will continue to be owned and operated by those public entities. JM Prophecies Brain Care will enter into multiple public/private operating partnerships for JM Prophecies value-adding properties, businesses, and services. Wherever possible, JM Prophecies will seek to acquire land adjacent to or surrounding the public properties.

Step 5 is summarized in figure 1 below and the subject of chapter 4.

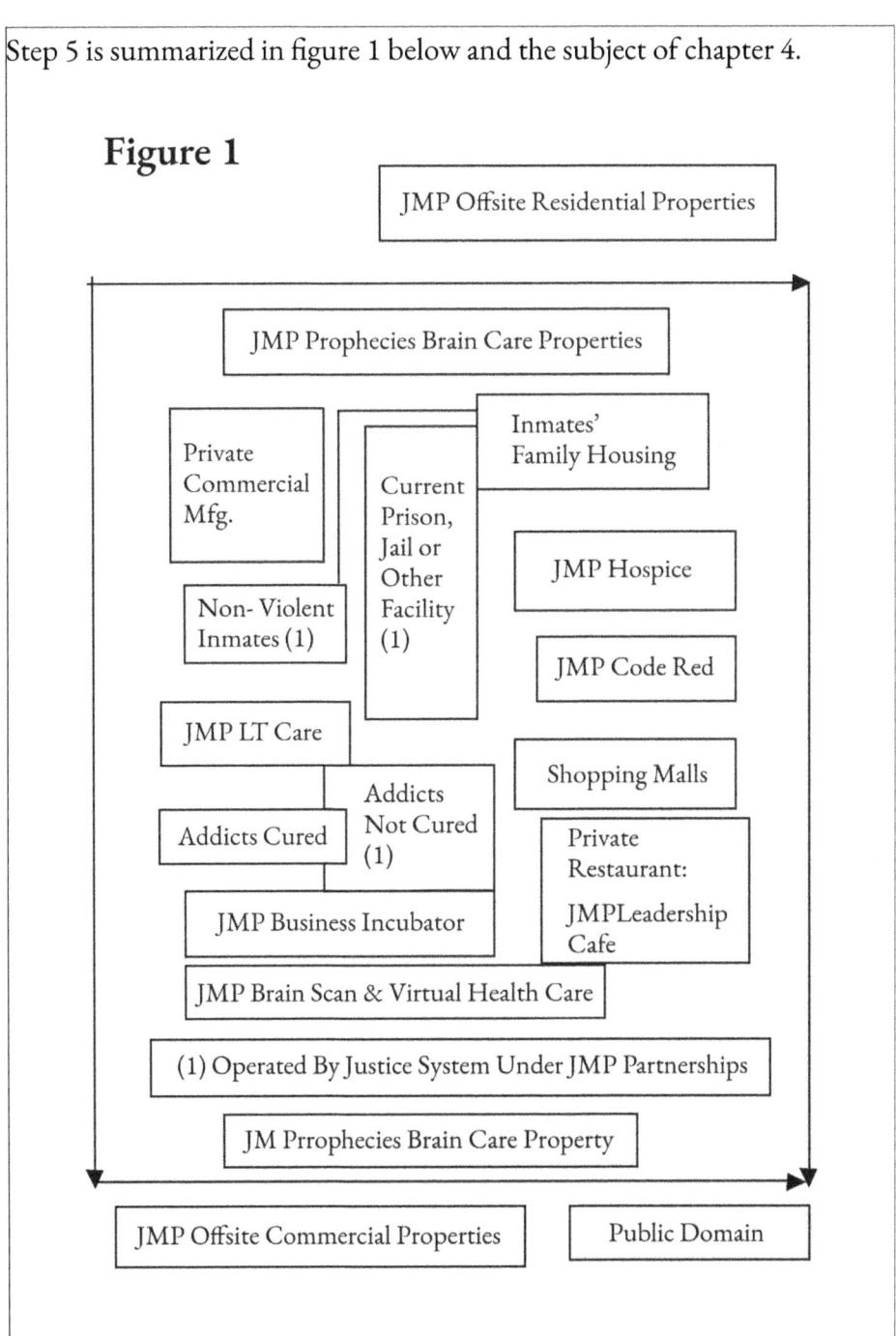

CHAPTER 2

THE THREE PENDULUMS OF A SOCIETY

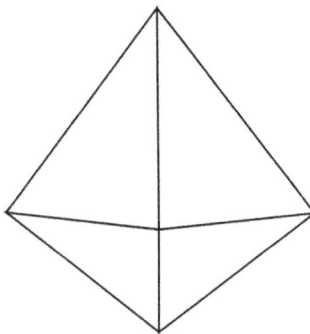

If you have never visited St. Augustine, Florida, you should. St. Augustine is the oldest city in the US, founded in September 1565. If you have been to St. Augustine, you undoubtedly gazed at the magnificent architecture of the main buildings at the corner of Cathedral Place and St. George, which still form the center of the city today. Two of the original buildings are the Governor's House, the political foundation of the city, and the cathedral basilica, the civil society foundation of the city. The treasury on the plaza, the economic foundation of the city, was added in the 1920s.

These three foundations still form the three parts of a modern society today. I call these *the three pendulums of a society*. I refer to these three foundations as pendulums because they are constantly swinging back and forth independently in three dimensions. A representation of this dynamic is shown in figure 2 below.

FIGURE 2

**The 3 Pendulums of a Society - They Are Constantly
Swinging Pendulums In Dynamic 3 Dimensions**

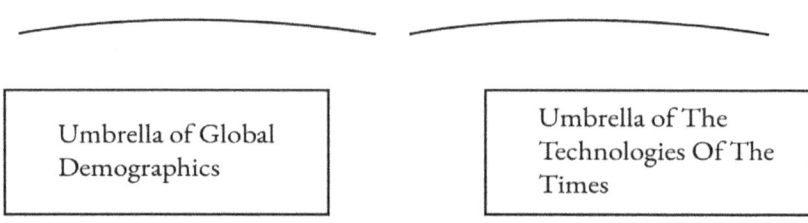

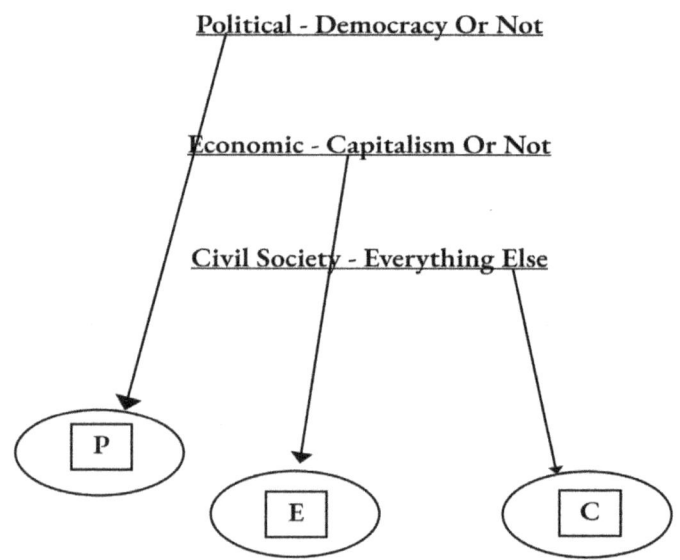

THE UMBRELLAS OF GLOBAL DEMOGRAPHICS AND THE TECHNOLOGIES OF THE TIMES

The three pendulums exist and swing under *the umbrella of global demographics* and *the umbrella of the technologies of the times*. Taken together, the study and analysis of (1) global demographics; (2) the technologies of the times; and (3) the three pendulums of a society form what I call the *headwaters of prophecy*, which can be used to predict the future. "Events to Happen, Things to Come, Learning to See the Future" is my leadership model to predict the future and is covered in chapter 3. In chapter 1, I discussed *prophecy must come before vision*. Studying, analyzing, and interjecting your own innate feel or intuition into the headwaters of *your* prophecies is the prerequisite work for you as a leader in order for you to establish and articulate your vision for your organization. This same process can be used by individuals to help establish their own life goals and paths to follow.

GLOBAL DEMOGRAPHICS

For a nation so caught up in immigration, it is disappointing to seldom see articles documenting a company or political body considering global demographics as part of any major decision process. Is any CEO or board of directors analyzing China's long-term demographics when determining their China strategy? China is approaching its demographic demise, and in spite of the Chinese Communist Party's desperate attempts to change their course, there is no fixing it. Our internal JM Prophecies demographic forecasts project that China and the US populations will crisscross by the end of this century at approximately 650 million people. We also forecast Florida will hold the largest population by state in the US by the end of the century, with sixty million people, approximating the then population and economy the size of Japan. How will China deal with its demographic demise? How will Japan? How will their contraction impact your company's Asian strategy? Just saying, "That is so far away, why bother?" is not an answer. These global demographic shifts impact far up the calendar before they are tabulated in census counts. How will the US and Florida prepare for a doubling and tripling, respectively, of their populations?

Current birth rates are dropping across the spectrum of modern societies. Modern birth control and contraceptives started this slide and are part of our society forever. China and the US are no exceptions. But there are two major differences in these two countries regarding birth rates that impact their overall populations. First, I believe the US birth rate will increase as the serfdoms of our times are unraveled in the US. Women wanting to become mothers has not fundamentally changed in the US. But economic and society pressures became too great to cope for a generational period. But this will change (the pendulums just keep swinging back and forth). China, however, has no such self-correcting pendulums. Wives in China increasingly regret ever getting married, let alone having more children. Second is the issue of immigration. People will never stop coming to the US. And, in varying degrees and directions of pendulum swings, the US will always continue to accept new immigrants. China will never benefit from immigration. Who wants to move to a communist society? Furthermore, it is only a matter of time before China begins to experience internal rebellions, which may end in a Balkans-style breakup into multiple countries.

THE TECHNOLOGIES OF THE TIMES

The three pendulums swing upward as new technologies are invented and tend to swing back as those new technologies become commonplace. Fissures arise among the three pendulum equilibriums when the individual pendulums adopt new technologies at significantly varying rates. We see this fissure today with big tech. Private industry adoption and integration of the internet, AI, and other electronic technologies have far surpassed our governments' adoption and integration at many levels.

WHICH PENDULUM SHOULD LEAD THE DEVELOPMENT OF THE TECHNOLOGIES OF THE TIMES?

For most of our country's history, our federal government has led the development of new technologies. In recent years, the federal government has slowed its investment in and development of new leading technologies. In order to maintain our global leadership for democratic pendulums, our federal government must regain that tip of the spear for new technology development. We must push that pendulum swing much farther out than currently exists. In 1941, the US Supreme Court established patent law doctrine that continues to this day through the Court's *flash of genius* doctrine. Our country needs a flash of genius renaissance. How could such a renaissance get started? We suggest the following action points:

- **Reimagine and reposition the federal laboratories. Add/reposition federal laboratories for advanced biologics, proteins, and polymers:** We believe biologics, including human and nonhuman cell therapies, synthetic proteins, and polymer inventions, will lead the flash of genius moments in the twenty-first century.

- **Prioritize the invention of synthetic raw materials**: Eventually, we will deplete naturally occurring and mined raw materials. This century should lead nothing less than an entire rewrite of the periodic table of elements.

- **Reimagine and reposition the nation's land grant universities**: We must stop and reverse urban sprawl, which has created the serfdoms of our times. Eliminating these serfdoms should include leadership by the nation's land grant universities. These land grant universities once led the economic development of rural America. What better mission than to double down on that history?

- **Creation of an intellectual society**: Education must lead the way into the twenty-first century. Rather than dumbing down K–12, we should advance *everyone's* education and intellect through a lifelong learning initiative.
  - An intellectual society isn't just an educated populace. It is a society of ideas. It is a society of flashes of genius, which become the future technologies of the times.

- **Global demographics of aging**: The study of global demographics includes not only the number of citizens but also their ages. The aforementioned declining fertility rates are and will be accompanied by the aging of populations and societies. Whichever country learns to maximize the contributions of its aging population will likely win the global demographics umbrella puzzle of prophecy. As shown in exhibit 1 below, the population distribution of the US has historically been a pyramid distribution, with more younger people positioned at the bottom of the pyramid supporting elder generations above them. However, the US age distribution has now become a pillar shape, with each age group on its own. Most countries of the world are experiencing similar pillar shifts. We simply must help our aging citizens stay productive longer. Predicting the future absolutely must consider the effects of global aging populations.

- **Any leader who is not coming up with their own prophecies regarding the future impact of global populations aging on their organization is not doing their job!**

Exibit 1

FROM PYRAMID TO PILLAR

A CENTURY OF CHANGE OF THE UNITED STATES POPULATION

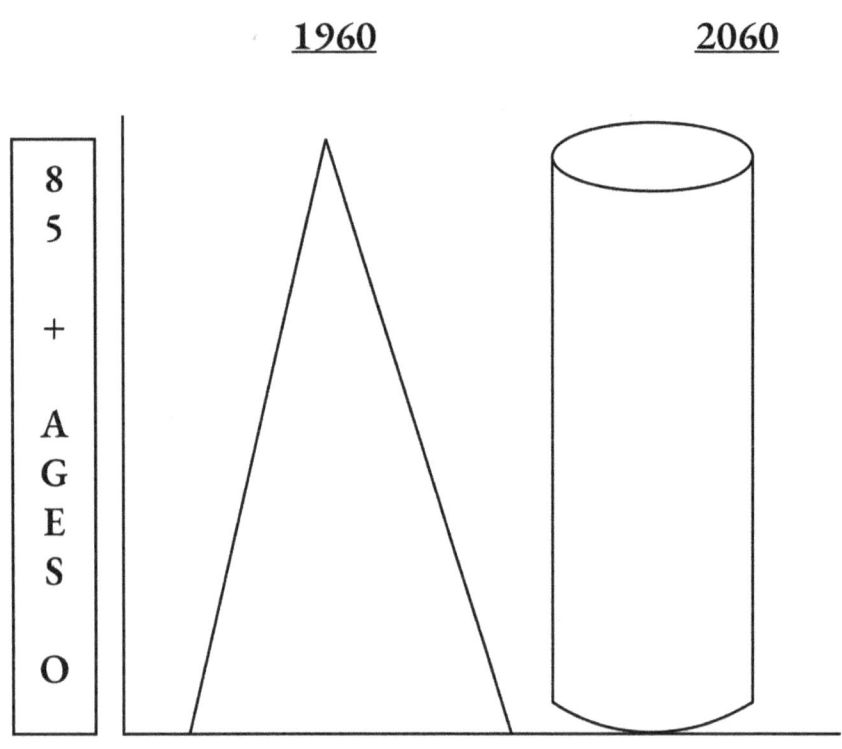

- **Creation of the nautical nation:** Unlike island nations like Great Britain and Japan, our country never developed the DNA of a nautical nation. We need to add that DNA to the body of our nation. We could begin this quest with:
- Development of the Caribbean: This is a great area of opportunity that can no longer be ignored.
    - Island building: Taking back and creating usable land mass from rising sea levels.
    - Hawaii becomes the center of commerce in the Pacific: Hawaii can become the economic, political, and cultural center of the Pacific. This opportunity currently exists due to:
        - the coming demographic demise of Eastern Asia.
        - virtual and remote working will continue to lead a reverse migration from large urban centers to areas with better qualities of life—an area of great strength for Hawaii.
        - a complete redo of global supply chains from Eastern Asia to competing countries in Asia and the Western Hemisphere.

POLITICAL PENDULUM—DEMOCRATIC OR NOT

Political Pendulum under a democratic society: Political pendulums in a democracy swing freely, often resulting in chaos over the short term as its citizens exercise their democratic rights. It's these chaotic swings that give democracies great strength over time as compared to communist and dictator pendulums. Centrally controlled forms of government simply continue in the same dictated direction, with no natural process to provide corrections.

US FEDERAL GOVERNMENT

AI for government services: Benjamin Franklin's famous insight "a republic if you can keep it," is still great insight for all of us today. As previously discussed, fissures open among the three pendulums when they adopt new technologies at significantly different rates. I don't think it is an overstatement to say our political pendulum is struggling today. I believe this is largely due to the slow adoption of the technologies of our times by our government and other nonprofit sectors. For example. if you add together the number of US senators and House representatives, the president, vice president, Supreme Court, plus a few cabinet members, it adds up to around six hundred people. Can six hundred people really provide leadership for 350–650 million people in a third or fourth industrial revolution society without advanced feedback and two-way information systems?

Other fissure examples include a general dissatisfaction with the federal, state, and local governments as well as other nonprofit institutions and services. Whether it is defunding the police, election recalls at all levels, disputed election results, teachers' unions at odds with parents, or letting homeless populations camp in front of multimillion-dollar homes, the US populace is not happy with its government and other nonprofit vendors. When your customers would rather pay for expensive alternatives than get their already provided products for free (parents paying for private K–12 education), you had better believe you are in trouble as a provider of services. We are deep in a classic example of what happens when one pendulum gets too technologically far behind. For this reason, JM Prophecies will focus on building AI systems for government and other nonprofit services to help these organizations and institutions close those fissures in the three pendulums.

Budgets and spending: It's hard to select the top issue of our government's struggles today. But we believe it is the absolutely out-of-control budget process. Accordingly, developing AI systems for governmental budgeting for a republic will be a priority for us.

Monetary policy: Monetary policy has become the looked-to salvation of our budget and spending woes. However, there are limits to this salvation. In spite of wishful thinking, this reliance on monetary policy will eventually come to an end. We only hope it ends before we squander the US dollar's reserve currency status. All crude oil sales around the world are settled in US dollars. An unintended detrimental consequence of green energy will be to weaken the US dollar's de facto world reserve currency status.

- **Cryptocurrencies**: Any discussion of monetary policy today combined with prophecy must necessarily include a position on cryptocurrencies. Our position at JM Prophecies regarding cryptocurrencies is best summarized by repeating Justice Antonin Scalia's quote: "some very good people have some very bad ideas."

Taxation Policies for the Fourth Industrial Revolution The complexity of the US economy and society has surpassed the capability of the country's early-twentieth-century taxing system to fund the government. We recommend the following additions to the current taxation systems.

- **Adopt a deficit reduction tax instead of raising interest rates.** When the inevitable shift in monetary policy and increase in interest rates come, we recommend the Federal Reserve be granted the authorization for charging fees instead of raising interest rates, equal to what the increase in interest rates would be, and applying those fees directly against outstanding Treasury securities. The Federal Reserve issuing unprecedented levels of debt and then raising interest rates would be akin to credit card companies getting credit card customers into high debt levels and then increasing interest rates when they cannot even pay their debt at low rates.

- **Taxing the underground and illegal economies**: We must begin taxing the country's underground and illegal economies. Not only will this help raise taxes to address our budget deficits, but it can also begin to make these illegal economies less lucrative for their participants.

- **Time for a national sales tax**: I believe the best way to tax the underground and illegal economies is to institute a national sales tax. Paid sales taxes could be treated as a credit against income taxes paid by both individuals and corporations when they subsequently file their annual income tax returns. This approach would also serve to tax corporations and individuals that currently pay little or no income taxes.

STATE AND LOCAL GOVERNMENTS

Competition among state and local governments: Political pendulums also exist and swing at the state and local government levels. Competition among states and local governments is important for effective political policy.

POLITICAL PENDULUMS UNDER A NONDEMOCRATIC SOCIETY

Political pendulums under a nondemocratic society, such as communism or a dictatorship, do *not* swing freely, and as a result, they always eventually fail.

ECONOMIC PENDULUM—CAPITALISTIC OR NOT

The role of capitalism in the third and fourth industrial revolutions: Much has been written and discussed recently regarding the role of capitalism in our country today and into the future. We believe there have always been and will continue to be the following three lead roles for capitalism in a democratic society:

- **Maximizing and expanding the technologies of the times**: One of three primary responsibilities for capitalism is to maximize and expand the technologies of the times. Examples are building global shipping from sailing to steam to diesel ships; building out the internet; building a commercial nuclear energy industry.

- **Identifying and creating revenue streams for all stakeholders**: While maximizing and expanding the technologies of the times, capitalism must identify and create new revenue streams for all stakeholders. Note: this responsibility may or may not result in profitable enterprises. In fact, history is filled with examples of early adoption of new technologies that generated significant revenues but did not generate net income. These disruptive technologies will later become more common and generate net profits.

- **Identifying and creating net income opportunities for shareholders**: After new technologies begin to get past their disruptive stages, they then become adopted and maximized by investors and shareholders who require net income to invest. It is also the role of capitalism to make income in the long term for remaining shareholders. Many of the technologies' inventors, early adopters, and early stakeholders will have long ago exited by this stage, already on to their next flash of genius.

Monitoring swings of the economic pendulum is critical for investors, especially contrarian investors. Investors optimize their returns when they jump on the economic pendulum at the height of its upward peak and position themselves on the inside of the pendulum to reap the rewards of the swing back in the opposite direction.

Smart investors also look for fissures among the three pendulums, which become inevitably at least partially filled in by the economic pendulum.

CIVIL SOCIETY PENDULUM—EVERYTHING ELSE

The civil society pendulum includes everything that is not political or economic. The most important segments of the civil society pendulum are discussed below.

- **Education**: Down the street from the cathedral basilica in St. Augustine sits the oldest schoolhouse in America. It is a small wooden shack, but it may well be the most popular selfie attraction in St. Augustine. There is something about education that captivates people. Humans are naturally curious beings. At JM Prophecies, we categorize education into three parts: (1) knowledge accumulation; (2) credentialing; and (3) flash of genius moments.

    ◦ **Moving toward an intellectual society**: An intellectual society creates ideas that advance the society. These advances build the society in a step function progression, not a linear progression. Moving toward the intellectual society is our area of great importance and focus at JM Prophecies. We plan to launch and operate both physical and virtual incubators across the multiple industries we are most focused upon.

- **Religion and places of worship (or not)**: The Spanish founders of St. Augustine understood the importance of including religion in their society. Unfortunately, the importance of religion has waned in American society over the centuries since St. Augustine was founded. This declining importance of religion has also led to a significant decline in the belief and appreciation of a spiritual foundation for our society. We at JM Prophecies understand the importance of a spiritual foundation. We refer to this spirituality as a higher power. Belief in and living under a higher power philosophy means more than belief in a single religion. We wrap a higher power into our overall decision-making process, which will be discussed in our future published works.

- **Society of laws**: A society's network of federal, state, and local laws and regulations comprise a major part of the civil society pendulum. Breaking the laws of a civil society often results in dropping to the bottom of the wealth inequality pyramid. Adverse behaviors, such as breaking society's laws, can have common problems and, we believe, can also have common solutions. For this reason, we have formed JM Prophecies Brain Care to focus on these common problems and provide solutions. Most adverse behaviors began with a traumatic experience. Trauma often comes from some form of abuse, often at an early age. Trauma can also begin with the sudden loss of a loved one through divorce, death, addiction of a family member, or many other traumatic experiences.

- **Communication platforms for coming together**: Communications have always been a major part of any society. Communications have advanced from verbal languages to written languages to constantly advancing electronic communication devices. Advancing electronic communication devices, when properly channeled, can help invert the wealth inequality pyramid and are a focus for us.

- **Urban versus rural—eliminating the serfdoms of our times**: The large urban areas of the world have become the serfdoms of our times. We believe this trend must be reversed and the serfdoms unraveled if we are to invert the wealth inequality pyramid.
- **Defeating climate change**: perhaps the greatest challenge ever to humanity. Compare the pre-human planetary footprint to the current day planetary footprint and you can understand why climate change is real and why a desperate attempt at reducing greenhouse gas emissions will never approach the scale of what human activities have done over thousands of years to the natural carbon, photosynthesis, and hydration cycles and ecosystems.

FISSURES IN THE THREE PENDULUM SWINGS

When the three pendulums are not in sync with one another, they form what we call fissures among the three pendulums. They each also then attempt to fill in the fissures and compensate for another slow-swinging or out-of-sync pendulum. These fissures can force people to the bottom of the wealth inequality pyramid, but they can also open up opportunities for those who can identify and take advantage of them.

POSITIONING YOURSELF ON THE INSIDE OF A PENDULUM

Swings in the three pendulums create opportunities for contrarian investing. Contrarian investors try to time their entry at the top of pendulum swings and position themselves on the inside of the pendulum so they can see what is coming at them rather than investing in the past.

THE POWER OF CONTRARIAN THOUGHT AND STRATEGY FOR THE CIVIL SOCIETY PENDULUM

It is no secret that our country is split approximately fifty-fifty on just about any topic you select to debate. Whenever you see fifty-fifty probability distributions among large sample sizes over broad topics and over a long period of time, those probabilities indicate that *events to happen*, as discussed in chapter 3, are nowhere near mature and are subject to tremendous influence from *things to come*. Therefore, you can actually alter the future by driving your 180-degree contrarian stake in the ground and saying, "No, conventional thought is entirely wrong, and here is the real answer." This takes courage and conviction of thought.

THE VELOCITY OF PENDULUM SWINGS

In the monetary policy world, it is a well-known axiom that increases in the money supply have a velocity of money effect, meaning an increase in say $1 billion has a multiplier effect on the economy, resulting in multiples of the original infusion of money. Similarly, the three pendulums of a society swing back and forth with velocity. The velocity's coefficient varies with the height and time duration of the pendulum swings. If you sit idly by and do not attempt to predict the future, you will run the risk of being overrun by pendulum swings. But, even worse, if you bet on a pendulum swing and bet wrong, your loss will be a multiple of your original bet.

INEQUALITY PYRAMIDS FOR PUBLIC POLICY

There are many components of society that drive the civil society pendulum. Parts of these components are addressed in this book. The other components will be addressed in subsequent books. A list of these additional components expressed in terms of the wealth inequality pyramid for your consideration are included in the following figure 3.

Inequality Pyramids for Public Policy

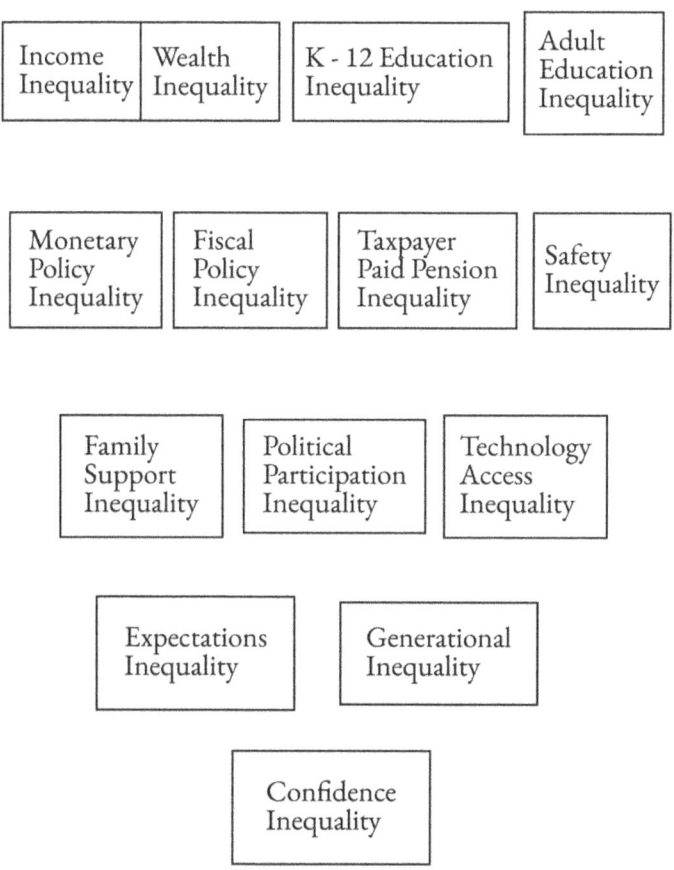

Figure 3
Inequality Pyramids for Public Policy

CHAPTER 3

EVENTS TO HAPPEN—THINGS TO COME

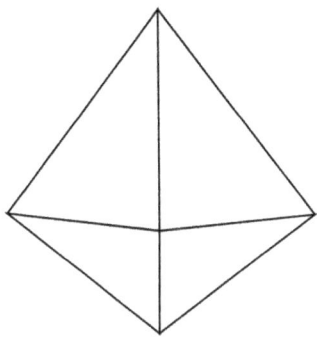

EVENTS TO HAPPEN

Nothing happens spontaneously: All events to happen in the future of any kind will come as the result of a series of connected past chain of events. Some events in the future will come as a result of a series of events that connected them only recently. Many events in the future will come as the result of a series of linked events that will then extend back decades, centuries, and even many millennia in the case of ancient climate change.

Events to happen are future events that *will happen* no matter what anyone does. Their past chain of events has already dictated these events will occur. They cannot be changed or prevented.

THINGS TO COME

Things to come are future events that will happen, but we still have the opportunity to alter their outcomes through actions we take now and in the future.

LEARNING TO SEE AND ALTER THE FUTURE

You can always be the smartest person in the room because you can learn to see *events to happen* and sometimes alter the future for *things to come*. Your path to always being the smartest person in *your* room can be paved by following the process set forth below.

Monitor and analyze the three headwaters of your prophecies: In previous chapters, we discussed the components of the three headwaters of prophecy. These three headwaters are:

- global demographics
- the technologies of the times
- the three pendulums of a society

The first step in learning to see and alter the future is to continually monitor and analyze the three headwaters of prophecy. It is important to monitor and analyze the data and events that will most impact you and your organization. It is not necessary or even possible to analyze all global data and events. For example, I do not study data or events in Cuba, Thailand, or Turkey. Others might have need to study these countries' demographics. I do not try to pick which green energy fuels will replace fossil fuels. Although this question is important to many people, I just do not feel confident in making any credible prophecies in this area at this time. After your analysis of what is most important to you and your organization is complete, perform the following steps discussed below.

Publish your prophecies: After you have made your conclusions, you must publish your prophecies for at least your organization to see and read. Publish your prophecies in two types, as follows:

Type I prophecies—global events to happen: These are your predictions of major events that will shape the future of the world from the date of your predictions through future generations. Remember, these events *will* happen, and nothing can be done to prevent them from happening.

Type II prophecies—regional, local, and industry specific events to happen that will impact you and your organization: These are your predictions of the major events that will shape the future of your life and the organization you lead. Again, remember, these events *will* happen, and nothing can be done to prevent them from happening.

Establish and publish your vision: After you have concluded and published your type I and type II prophecies, establish your vision for the organization you lead and for your own personal life and your family. Openly publish that vision as the beginning and basis of your organization's future quests, strategies, and customary business planning.

Publish your story and be the chief storyteller: In order to best articulate your prophecies to others, you must develop your story and be your own best storyteller. As you tell your story to others, be sure to encourage them to develop their own type I and type II prophecies for their personal lives and to test if they agree with yours. Obviously, not everyone will agree on the same prophecies. Just because these events to happen are going to occur and cannot be stopped or altered does not mean we will all predict them the same with one hundred percent certainty or accuracy.

My favorite movies and books tell the story of the Battle of Midway. If you have not studied this famous battle that changed the course of World War II in the Pacific, you should. This battle is a classic example of (1) believing in false prophecies—Japanese Admiral Nagumo, (2) establishing serendipity pools—American Admiral Nimitz, and (3) decision-making under uncertainty—American Navy personnel at all levels. The Chinese military studies the Battle of Midway with delusions of how they could have won that battle. Their wishful thinking carries the same fatal flaw that Japanese Admirals Yamamoto and Nagumo had. In war, once the first shot is fired, all carefully conceived plans and strategies are worthless. The United States will never be defeated militarily because the three pendulums of American society also swing freely with the US military.

Publish your vision, strategies, and business plan: After you have your type I and type II prophecies firmly in your mind, the vision, strategies, and business plans will come easily to you and to others with more confidence and conviction than before. In the Battle of Midway, once the Americans knew that the Japanese code name "AF" was their code for Midway, all following plans and activities came with great confidence for the American Navy. But the plan to confirm the meaning of AF was due to the prophecy of American intelligence officers and personnel that AF was indeed Midway. Having that belief and prophecy with scant information led to eventual victory in the Pacific.

Establish your serendipity pools: As much as we would all love to solve all the problems of the world, obviously we cannot. But what we can do is establish what I call *serendipity pools*—those areas of critical interest to us and the organizations we lead. We can use those serendipity pools to focus our time, money, and mindshare on opportunities arising from events coming through our serendipity pools. Serendipity pools can be closely related to what we currently do, or they could monitor chains of historical events for areas we are not currently involved in. For example, working with aging-out foster care organizations is an area of immediate serendipity management for us. Conversely, although I am a novice of the energy industry, I am interested in monitoring it for future opportunities and weaknesses in the country's eventual energy policy in order to exploit those opportunities and weaknesses by positioning on the inside of the green energy pendulum at its highest peak.

Corporate partnerships are a great example of establishing serendipity pools. Selecting partners wisely is critical for any organization, especially young companies. At JM Prophecies, we plan to engage in corporate partnerships in (1) financial services, (2) information technology, and (3) medical centers, as well as other partners for JM Prophecies Brain Care. As contrarian investors, we currently have no plans to ever engage with a media industry partner, deciding instead to go it alone in media.

Confronting type II events to happen and channeling things-to-come decisions through your serendipity pool pathways: If possible, it is best to confront future type II events to happen within your serendipity pools and to also make your things-to-come decisions within your serendipity pools.

Power of positioning: Positioning is so important. For the Greeks, it was the Thermopylae Pass in 480 BC; for the Union Army in the American Civil War, it was the high ground at Gettysburg; and for the invasion of Europe, it was the beaches of Normandy for the Allies.

Serendipity pools can be geographic or not. At JM Prophecies, we have selected Florida and Hawaii as our Thermopylae Pass twin pillars. But our corporate partners will not all be in Florida or Hawaii; many will, but some will not. Obviously, serendipity pools can be managed virtually.

JM Prophecies Corporation Serendipity Pools and "Things to Come Pathways" Example

Figure 4 below demonstrates how we at JM Prophecies Corporation think about positioning.

FIGURE 4

JM Prophecies Corporation Serendipity Pools and Pathways for "Things To Come"

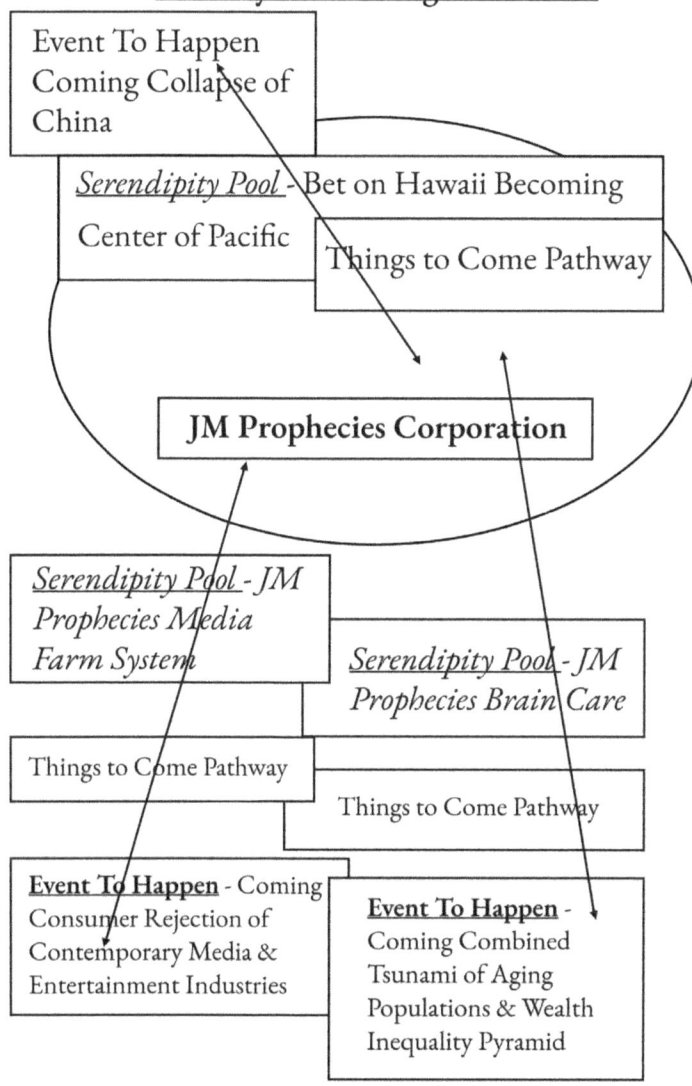

Embrace your higher power and learn to follow the signs: Long before we ever contemplated forming JM Prophecies, our family observed for years that signs from a higher power really do come and are there for us to see and follow if we only learn to look and act when we do see them. We have also observed that what I refer to as the Hall of Souls can and does occasionally give us signs that help guide us through our long-term decision-making. We have observed these signs come to us when we are helping others, but they do not come to us if we do not help others. To its detriment, our country has become increasingly secular. It is beyond the scope of this book for me to recommend others follow our Hall of Souls philosophy, but I suggest you at least consider these thoughts in your personal lives.

Decision-making under uncertainty: The final step in learning to alter the future is to become a star in decision-making under uncertainty. This is a skill that is not hard to learn if followed through a structured process. The key attributes of our process are as follows:

- **Making the right decision 100 percent of the time**: Because you have stacked the deck in your favor through the above process, you should be able to make the right call one hundred percent of the time with only ten to fifteen percent of the information during your daily major decision-making process.

- **Probability analysis and payoff outcomes**: When you are making your daily decisions at work or in life, apply classic probability analysis and payoff outcomes in your decision-making.

- **Decision-making is like playing poker**: Decision making under uncertainty is like playing poker. Follow the rules listed below during your daily decision-making process:

- Make certain it's a game you want to play at the time and with the players at the table.

- Play the hand you have, not the hand you wish you had.

- Decision-making is an incremental process. You do not need to make every decision at once; make them incrementally. It's a process. Just paying to see the next card or not is a decision.

- If you believe you have the winning hand, *always* bet big. You may not actually have the winning hand, but if you believe you do, always bet big. In poker, you do not get many big hands. The same holds true in business and our personal lives; we don't get many big opportunities in life, so we must pursue them when they come along.

- Every decision creates a new hand. The deck is constantly being reshuffled after every decision.

- Learn to recognize when you are being bluffed so you don't fold winning hands. Have the courage to stay in toe to toe when the bluffer gets desperate and ratchets up the bet.

Create and follow a feedback loop and repeat the above processes. Ask yourself the following questions as you create and follow your feedback loop:

Are your prophecies still valid and unchanged? Just because events to happen will happen with a hundred percent certainty, that doesn't mean our predictions or prophecies will be a hundred percent accurate. We may be wrong, and we may realize our errors as more of the chain of events come to pass. Admirals Yamamoto and Nagumo both could have and should have changed their attack plans due to events leading up to the Battle of Midway, but they did not.

Have the three pendulums of a society changed? Monitoring this part of your prophecy headwaters is critical. Changes in the chains of events can come rapidly and often reveal insights previously unknown or errors in predictions.

Does your vision need to be revised or embellished? Changes in your prophecies may require adjustment to your vision.

Does your story need to be revised or embellished? Changes in your prophecies and vision may require adjustments to your story.

Do your strategies or business plan need to be revised or embellished? Changes in your prophecies and vision may require adjustments to your detailed strategies or business plan.

PROPHECY BEFORE VISION

CHAPTER 4

LINKED PROBLEMS AND SOLUTIONS

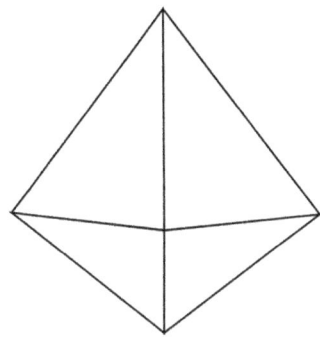

Any leader of any organization in the US must, both as a citizen and as the leader of their organization, be deeply concerned with the impact on our neighborhoods and broader communities from the negative consequences of crime, drugs, mental illness, and poverty. To simply turn a blind eye and believe these consequences will never impact their organization is being shortsighted. These combined problems are getting worse every day, and unless we act soon with new and productive strategies, they can overwhelm our civil society pendulum. These problems and issues are diverse, much like the proverbial ten-thousand-layer onion. In order to decide what to do, we first must start with an analysis of the numbers to gain an understanding of the enormity of the task at hand but also the enormity of the opportunity to truly move our country forward both economically and socially. A numbers overview is provided below.

CRIMES

Number of total crimes in the US:[1] 120 million

Number of violent crimes in the US:[1] 24 million

Total cost of crime in the US:[1] $2.6 trillion

Total cost of crime in the US as percentage of GDP: 10 percent

PRISONS AND PRISONERS

Number of prisons and facilities in the US:[2]

- state prisons: 1,833
- federal prisons: 110
- juvenile correctional facilities: 1,772
- local jails: 3,134
- immigration detention facilities: 218
- Indian country jails: 80

Annual number of new prisoners in the US:[2] 600,000

Number of incarcerations in the US:[2] 10.6 million

Annual churn rate of prisoners in the US:[2] 17.67 x

Non-crime-detained juveniles in the US:[2] 52,000

Number of current prisoners in the US:[2] 2.3 million

Number of former prisoners in the US:[2] 4.9 million

Number of felons in the US:[2] 19 million

Number with criminal record in the US:[2] 77 million

Number of family been in prison in the US:[2] 113 million

Number on probation in the US:[2] 3.6 million

Number on parole in the US:[2] 840,000

Number under justice system in the US:[2] 7 million

ALCOHOL AND DRUG ADDICTIONS

Those with at least one addiction in the US:[3] 21 million

Percentage treated for at least one addiction in the US:[3] 10 percent

Annual cost of addiction in the US:[3] $600+ billion

Total cost of addiction in the US as percentage of GDP: 2.9 percent

Percentage with disorder due to addiction in the US:[3] 20 percent

MENTAL ILLNESS

1. Forty percent of US adults struggle with mental health or substance use.[4]
2. The average delay between onset of mental illness symptoms and treatment is eleven years.[4]

According to the National Institute of Mental Health:

- In 2019, there were an estimated 51.5 million adults aged eighteen or older in the United States with Any Mental Illness (AMI). This number represented 20.6% of all U.S. adults.
- The prevalence of AMI was higher among females (24.5%) than males (16.3%).
- Young adults aged eighteen to twenty-five had the highest prevalence

of AMI (29.4%) compared to adults aged twenty-six to forty-nine (25.0%) and aged fifty and older (14.1%).

- The prevalence of AMI was highest among the adults reporting two or more races (31.7%), followed by White adults (22.2%). The prevalence of AMI was lowest among Asian adults (14.4%).[5]

According to the CDC - Centers for Disease Control and Prevention:

- Number of visits to physician offices with mental, behavioral, and neuro developmental disorders as the primary diagnosis: 56.8 million.

- Number of visits to emergency departments with mental disorders, behavioral, and neurodevelopmental as the primary diagnosis: 4.9 million.[6]

According to John Hopkins Medicine:

- Mental health disorders account for several of the top causes of disability in established market economies worldwide and include: major depression (also called clinical depression), manic depression (also called bipolar disorder), schizophrenia, and obsessive-compulsive disorder. [7]

HOMELESS

Number of homeless in the US: 1 million

Annual cost of homelessness in the US: $50 billion

Cost of homelessness in the US as percentage of GDP: 0.2 percent

It is incredibly difficult to accurately estimate the number of homeless in the US and also the cost. These difficulties are due to the fact that homelessness is actually a pipeline of groups of people at different stages in their plight. These pipeline's stages and groups are outlined below.

- Totally homeless—living unsheltered or in tents on city streets and parks.
- Homeless but sheltered in taxpayer or philanthropic funded shelters.
- Unemployed and/or addicted and freeloading with friends or others.
- Unemployed and/or addicted and freeloading with family members.
- Unemployed and/or addicted and living in RVs alongside a public road.
- Partially employed and/or addicted and living in RVs alongside a public road.
- Underemployed and living in RVs alongside a public road.

THE WORLD HAS BECOME TOO COMPLICATED FOR HUMANS TO LIVE IN IT

Much is being written about workers not going back to work after COVID-19 began subsiding and economies began recovering. I would agree with the conventional explanation: why would someone go back to work if the federal government continued paying them not to work? But I also believe there is something else going on here. During our discussions with homeless folks in our Homeless Interview Tours, a common theme kept coming through. People had just given up. They couldn't take real life anymore and had accepted any fate that lay before them rather than continue to fight back in a no-win life scenario. I believe this is the main reason masses of people are not returning to work. It's also why there is tremendous pushback from virtual workers not returning to the office. Many will quit before they ever go back into an office.

When I finally left the eight-to-five world as an employee to launch JM Prophecies Corporation, I started doing what every entrepreneur does to launch their business. I started with building my infrastructure from scratch. I hadn't upgraded my cell phone for six years, so I bought and converted to a new cell phone. My wife needed a new phone, so we went together. When we bought our phones, we were told the seller couldn't help us convert our phones because of too much legal liability from people losing their data if the seller helped them convert. So, my wife and I both left the store with new phones but unsure if we could convert our old data. Sure enough, no matter what we tried, we couldn't get our new phones to work. We set pride aside and went back to the store. Fortunately, we then were helped by a transferred store manager who was quite disappointed to hear about our previous experience and helped us transfer our new phones. (The first thing she had to do was replace the SIM cards in both phones.)

After spending a week converting our phones, next up was to buy a new laptop, get going on a website-development strategy, and select and sign an office space lease. We went to a top store and got my shiny new laptop. I got it home, and after a couple days wanted to have my first Zoom board call. Well, the speakers didn't work. So, I took the computer back to the store. The seller couldn't fix it at the store and needed to send it back to the manufacturer. I said, "Okay, I'll buy another to work with in the meantime."

I was told the store had no more of that model and didn't expect to receive any more under their quota. I then bought the next lower model, and it worked fine. Three weeks later, I got a text from the store saying they needed to talk. The story ended with the computer not being fixable, and they gave me my money back.

In an earlier encounter, we wanted to buy an upright pool heater so I could work by the pool during chilly hours. We found the "perfect" heater and were not deterred by "some assembly required" but were reluctant about the "Made in China" stamp. We had no alternative, so we bought it. When we started to assemble it, we discovered there was no base. Once again, we were burned by buying junk from China that never works. We returned the heater and vowed to never again buy anything made in China. Unfortunately, we have found that vow hard, if not impossible, to keep when purchasing anything online.

None of the above series of events materially altered our lives. But stringing the chain of events together along with other similar events made me realize that everyone around the globe just assumes (both businesses and consumers) that when they make or purchase a finished product, component, or subassembly, what they are buying works and will fit together seamlessly. Well, we are all finding out this is simply not true. Just-in-time supply chains from China and elsewhere have broken down everywhere. As a result, people are giving up working and living in that world and opting for a simpler life and world, even if it means a dramatically reduced standard of living.

IMPACT ON OUR NEIGHBORHOODS AND CIVIL SOCIETY

The above numbers and metrics are staggering. There is no sense in even trying to sugarcoat where we are. It is impossible for the civil society pendulum to absorb all of the events measured by these data points and continue to function properly. There is a growing awareness of prophecy among professionals working in the judicial system, health care, politics, and communities that massive changes are necessary. But where does one begin? The ten-thousand-layer onion is messy. It smells and often brings us to tears.

In my opinion, the first layer of the onion to peel back is separating the groups of above individuals discussed in this chapter from our neighborhoods and helping them separately. The previously discussed concentric villages in Chapter 1 envisioned in JM Prophecies Brain Care is our approach. If someone has a better approach, we would love to hear about it.

MINORITY RIGHTS BUT MAJORITY RULE

More than ninety percent of the US population follows all the laws and regulations. Less than ten percent commit crimes, become addicts, and harm their family, neighbors, and neighborhoods. It is time to become a more civilized society and help the minority become happy and successful members of our country. But it's also not fair to the majority to continue to incur the wrath of the less than ten percent.

ISOLATION = ABUSE = BOTTOM OF WEALTH INEQUALITY PYRAMID

Unfortunately, our American society is becoming more isolated. Isolation is a form of abuse. We see it every day. And it's not just COVID-19. Our entire judicial system is predicated on isolation. We don't buy much from entrepreneurs or private small business owners who know us, let alone treat us with any special service. Social media takes mindshare and isolates us, in spite of claims of bringing us together. We argue over everything, and most of the arguing is over nothing that matters.

We are becoming a nation of talkers and make-believers, no longer a society of doers and action. Youth jobs are hard to get. Jobs that would pull them together under a broader umbrella. Forget summer late-night baseball under the lights. Forget summer agriculture jobs: de-tasseling corn, walking beans, construction jobs (does anyone reading this book even know what walking beans means)?

THE FINANCIAL OPPORTUNITY FOR OUR COUNTRY

We believe the financial opportunity for our country by taking a JM Prophecies Brain Care approach dwarfs any other single opportunity that exists. We believe if you add up the following opportunities, it totals approximately twenty to forty percent of the GDP annually:

- Out-of-pocket costs of aforementioned events already being spent
- Lost opportunity for income and wealth accumulation for above groups

- Cost to others in their neighborhoods for acts committed
- Lost opportunity for income and wealth by others in their neighborhoods from acts committed
- Velocity of money on top of all of the above
- Next generation benefit from all of the above

Assuming a US GDP of $22.2 trillion[8] and total annual federal government spending of $7 trillion,[8] respectively, twenty to forty percent of the GDP would equal $4.4–8.8 trillion (this approximates the entire federal government annual cash outlays).

Assuming an annual federal government financial deficit of $3.6 trillion[8] and a total federal deficit of $28.4 trillion,[8] a concentric villages approach at a full-run rate could pay off the entire national debt in approximately six years on a weighted average run rate basis.

THE FINANCIAL OPPORTUNITY FOR CRIMINALS

Much like the global wealth inequality pyramid in the legal economy, this same condition is paralleled in the illegal economy. Over the long term, most criminals end up badly. They either are killed or end up in prison, or both. Over the short term, the rank and file criminals and drug dealers don't fare any better. Say a street soldier makes $1,500 per week on a good week, so an annual tax-free cash gross of $78,000. But that is before jail time, down time, legal fees, and more. They can do better going legitimate, getting an education, and changing their life. They just need a chance and a protected environment for them and their families to change their lives—not to be thrown back out in the street, where the churning cycle never ends.

PROPHECY BEFORE VISION

We have the opportunity to break gangs and organized crime by eliminating their customers, foot soldiers, and future recruits.

CHAPTER 5

WHAT NOW? WHAT'S NEXT?

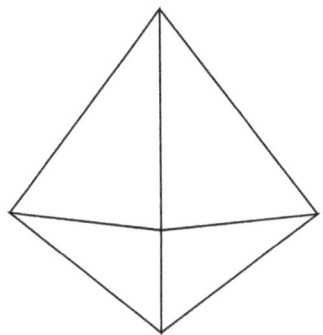

THE COMING ECONOMIC AND SOCIAL TSUNAMIS OF WEALTH INEQUALITY COMBINED WITH AGING POPULATIONS

The US, China, Japan, and most of the other countries of the world have two things in common: they all have economic and social tsunamis coming from wealth inequality combined with aging populations. If we do not solve these drains on our global societies, they will swamp us all in an endless downward spiral of unmet financial and social obligations. The civil society pendulum will no longer be capable of functioning.

DOWNWARD FINANCIAL SPIRAL

We have already discussed the financial perils of not resolving the wealth inequality pyramid. But we have not had this discussion through the lens of aging populations. Aging populations also need more and more support of all kinds, especially financial and labor. Not addressing the wealth inequality pyramid puts more downward spiral pressure on aging populations, and vice versa.

China's coming debt collapse: China's coming demographics and aging crises are going to be magnified and accelerated by its coming debt collapse. China's debt exceeds 250 percent of its GDP. Moreover, China's corporations are carrying the majority of that debt through the borrowing of state-owned enterprises. Does anyone really believe adequate loan loss reserves exist? Does anyone really believe many of those loans will ever be repaid?[9]

DOWNWARD SOCIAL SPIRAL

The downward spirals will not be limited to just money. If we do not raise the people out of the bottoms of the wealth inequality pyramid, there will not be enough physical bodies to care for our aging populations. The remaining care providers will become more and more fatigued and unable to care for our aging populations.

NUMBER OF WORKERS PER RETIREE

The average number of workers per retiree is dropping in most countries of the world. In the US, this ratio is dropping in no small part due to the growing number of people who have languished at the bottom of the wealth inequality pyramid and simply dropped out of the work force.

The average number of workers per retiree in China is dropping at a breathtaking pace. At JM Prophecies, we expect the ratio of the average number of workers per retiree in China to hit 1.0 sometime during the 2050–2060 decade under China's current retirement policies. Our current thinking is that an average ratio of 1.0 is the *breakup point*—the point at which a nation collapses and a Balkans-style breakup occurs. Obviously, if our predictions come true, the Chinese Communist Party will push every button and pull every lever at their disposal to prevent this from happening. We are already seeing these changes in policy taking place, such as now officially allowing a two-child family and raising the retirement age. But a two-child or more family in a Communist nation will mean nothing. And raising the retirement age with no value added for the retiree will bring its own new set of social challenges, negating any gain from an increased retiree ratio.

IT'S TIME TO MAKE 180-DEGREE CONTRARIAN BETS

Concentric villages as an economic development strategy: It is time to utilize underperforming populations languishing at the bottom of the wealth inequality pyramid as centers of economic growth and development. This can be accomplished by adopting the concentric villages of JM Prophecies Brain Care as a real estate development strategy and as a community economic development strategy.

WHAT IS OUR FUTURE TRANSPORTATION INFRASTRUCTURE STRATEGY?

A question I have for my readers is this: what do you believe should be our country's long-term transportation infrastructure strategy? The main points here are as follows:

- Assuming our population doubles in the twenty-first century, what should our strategy be?

- A bullet trains strategy versus more airports and air travel—this is an issue I am still grappling with. As of now, I believe bullet trains are not the best alternative for the US, and more airports and interstate highways (especially toll highways) are the better alternative. I have come to this conclusion after the following analysis.

I believe a country's transportation infrastructure strategy should include the following three goals:

1. Get passengers from point A to point B.
2. Promote economic development.
3. Help integrate cultures both domestically and across a country's borders.

My analysis concludes the following:

1. Bullet trains, much like airplanes, are meant to get passengers from one place to another fast. Speed is the main factor. However, bullet trains do not promote economic development along the rail lines because, by definition, there is no time allotted for stopping to develop the rail line communities.
2. Interstate highways promote economic development along their pathways, much like the slow railroads of the 1800s. If you want to see a great example of this phenomenon, just drive along Interstate 70 to Kansas City west from St. Louis. Interestingly, if you travel east from St. Louis along Interstate 64, there is hardly any economic development. I have observed this condition before. East St. Louis lies east of St. Louis, and people will not develop and also will not jump the serfdoms of our times. Interstate 64 east from St. Louis bears this out.

3. Bullet trains that cross country borders are fine because they can help integrate cross-country borders, cultures, and economies. This is why trains in Europe have been so successful for almost two centuries. China has built an impressive fast train system, but it can never cross its borders because its outbound passengers would never return.

CHAPTER 6

CASE STUDIES: LEARNING PROPHECY

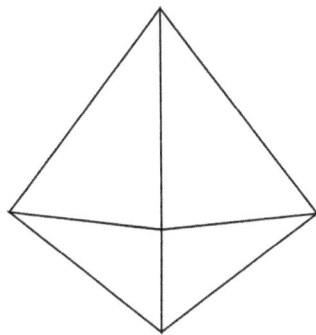

EXAMPLE CASE STUDIES

I have provided in this chapter a number of case studies designed to complete your training to learn how to see and alter the future.

Furthermore, in order to begin peeling back the ten-thousand-layer-onion, this chapter provides a series of hypothetical case studies to encourage thinking about public policy changes to peel the onion. In previous chapters, I made it perfectly clear that our JM Prophecies Brain Care approach is our solution. It would be pointless to restate our opinions in the case studies below. Therefore, I have structured each case study below for the reader to come to their own conclusions and recommendations, complete with space for notetaking during your reading. I welcome your feedback in whatever form you feel comfortable providing. I thank you in advance for your consideration and thoughts.

Case Study 1—Criminal Churn

Topic introduction: The US criminal churn rate approximates 17X annually. This level of repeat offenders is overwhelming our judicial system.

As a result, judges, prosecutors, and politicians are turning to ever more lenient prosecutorial strategies to lessen their caseloads (who can blame them? Jails, prosecutors, police, and judges are overwhelmed). How can the churn rate best be reduced?

Reader Topic Analysis

___

Reader Conclusions and Recommendations

___

Case Study 2—Defunding the Police

Topic introduction: Defunding the police is a topic of great debate. Using the data points presented in prior chapters, please argue both the side of yes (defund the police) and no (defunding the police is a detrimental concept and will only make matters worse).

Reader Topic Analysis

___

Reader Conclusions and Recommendations

___

Case Study 3—Mental Illness

Topic introduction: During the past several years, the trend has been to close traditional mental health care hospitals and institutions. This trend has arguably led to massive numbers of cases of mental illness not being diagnosed or treated. Please provide your analysis of where the country lies as related to mental health care, and also provide any recommendations you may have.

Reader Topic Analysis

___

Reader Conclusions and Recommendations

___

Case Study 4—Drug Addiction

Topic introduction: Imagine you are the parents of a twenty-year-old son. He started using drugs at the age of fifteen. Prior to that time, he was a great student, had many friends, and was admired by his younger brother and sister. He has now been a drug addict for five years. He dropped out of high school and has stolen from you many times to feed his addiction. He has been in and out of rehabilitation four times, each time coming out clean, but each time, he slipped back into addiction. You still love your son, but you and his siblings can no longer believe he will ever get clean. In truth, he knows you all expect him to fail, which is part of his repeated failures.

Now imagine you are in front of the judge hearing your son's case for stealing to feed his drug habit. The judge has just informed you about the facilities at JM Prophecies Brain Care. The judge is now asking your opinion regarding what sentence he should levy on your again-convicted son. What would you say and recommend?

Reader Topic Analysis

_____

Reader Conclusions and Recommendations

_____

Case Study 5—Homelessness

Topic introduction: You are a longtime owner of a beachfront house that you have loved for years. You paid $2 million for your house ten years ago. You had it appraised for a refinancing two years ago and now owe $4 million on a house that then appraised for $6 million. An encampment of approximately three hundred homeless people now surrounds your house, practically forcing you into staying inside your home, which no longer has access to the beach without walking through the encampment. A judge recently ruled the local police can move the encampment but only if they can be moved to suitable housing.

Imagine your city council is meeting that very night, and you have been asked by your neighborhood watch group to testify at the city council meeting. What would you say?

Reader Topic Analysis

_____

_____

Reader Conclusions and Recommendations

_____

Case Study 6—Neighborhood Gangs Recruiting Your Children

Topic introduction: Your son and daughter are both good high school students and never get into trouble. Over the last year, two competing criminal gangs have been recruiting both children to join their gang or face dire consequences. Both gangs are also recruiting your younger elementary school-age children, further threatening your older children in their overall recruitment of all your children. The leaders of both gangs and many gang members were recently arrested and convicted for multiple crimes. The judge's sentence hearing will be held next week. The prosecutors have asked you to testify at the sentencing hearing. What will you say?

Reader Topic Analysis

_____

Reader Conclusions and Recommendations

_____

Case Study 7—Prisoners' Futures

Topic introduction: You have been in prison for ten years. You are up for parole. If paroled, you can leave the prison under the oversight of a probation officer. You will have no job and nowhere to go. The parole board offers you the choice of staying in prison in JM Prophecies Brain Care concentric villages of squares or going free into the street. What would you ask regarding clarification about JM Prophecies Brain Care, and what would you do?

Reader Topic Analysis

Reader Conclusions and Recommendations

Case Study 8—Prisoners' Family Members

Topic introduction: You are the wife of a man currently in prison. He has been in prison for five years and has five years more to serve. His prison has entered into an agreement with JM Prophecies Brain Care. You will have the opportunity to move along with your children into the JM Prophecies Brain Care villages. What would you ask regarding clarification about JM Prophecies Brain Care, and what would you do?

Reader Topic Analysis

Reader Conclusions and Recommendations

___

Case Study 9—Entrepreneurs Relocating to a JM Prophecies Brain Care Village

Topic introduction: You are an entrepreneur and have identified a company you would like to purchase and become the CEO of, but you need external financing to complete the transaction. An affiliate of JM Prophecies has agreed to finance your acquisition but with the requirement you locate the company in a JM Prophecies set of concentric villages, which would place you and your employees next to a prison. What would you do?

Reader Topic Analysis

___

Reader Conclusions and Recommendations

___

Case Study 10—CEO Prophecy

Topic introduction: You have read this book and understand the power of prophecy before vision. What are your type I prophecies? What are your type II prophecies? How do you plan to publish your prophecies with your investors and board of directors? How will you articulate your updated vision to your employees?

Reader Topic Analysis

Reader Conclusions and Recommendations

Case Study 11—ESG Fund Manager

Topic introduction: You have read this book and understand the power of prophecy before vision. What are your type I prophecies? What are your type II prophecies? How will your prophecies alter your investment strategies, if at all?

Reader Topic Analysis

Reader Conclusions and Recommendations

Case Study 12—CEO—The Technologies of the Times

Topic introduction: What do you consider to be the technologies of the times? How do you plan for them for your organization?

Reader Topic Analysis

Reader Conclusions and Recommendations

Case Study 13—CEO Prophecy—Three Pendulum Fissures

Topic introduction: Do you believe there are any material fissures in the three pendulums of a society that will impact your organization? If yes, what are they?

Reader Topic Analysis

Reader Conclusions and Recommendations

Case Study 14—CEO Prophecy—Serendipity Pools

Topic introduction: You are the CEO of an international trading company. What serendipity pools and strategy are you planning to recommend to your senior management team?

Reader Topic Analysis

_____

Reader Conclusions and Recommendations

_____

Case Study 15—Marketing Senior Vice President—Prophecy

Topic introduction: You have read this book and understand the power of prophecy before vision. What are your type I prophecies? What are your type II prophecies? Your CEO has published his prophecies and has asked how you look at prophecy from a marketing perspective. How will you articulate your thoughts to your CEO?

Reader Topic Analysis

_____

Reader Conclusions and Recommendations

Case Study 16—CEO and Board of Directors—Prophecy for China

Topic introduction: With your collective strategy, decision, and direction, your company has made a big bet investing in China. You obviously disagree with JM Prophecies' strategy and James Michael Matthew's prophecies one and four. Why do you disagree? What will happen to your company if you bet wrong?

Reader Topic Analysis

Reader Conclusions and Recommendations

Case Study 17—CEO and Board of Directors—Prophecy for Green Energy Economy

Topic introduction: How do you see the future series of events playing out in the US and globally for the conversion of a fossil fuel, energy-based economy to a green energy economy? What serendipity pools have you positioned for the coming of a green energy economy? What bets are you considering for pendulum swings created by the conversion to a green energy economy? How are you positioning your company on the inside of the pendulum?

Reader Topic Analysis

Reader Conclusions and Recommendations

Case Study 18—CEO and Board of Directors—Prophecy—Aging Populations

Topic introduction: Have you published any prophecies regarding the pending aging of populations? If yes, what are they and why did you pick them? If not, why not?

Reader Topic Analysis

Reader Conclusions and Recommendations

Case Study 19—CEO and Board of Directors—Prophecy—Study and Analysis of Global Demographics

Topic introduction: Does your company have an established methodology and forecasting policy for monitoring, analyzing, and forecasting global demographics? If not, why not? If yes, what are they? Do you maintain an actuarial chain-link historical forecasting model? If not, why not? If yes, how accurate has it been in predicting the future?

Reader Topic Analysis

Reader Conclusions and Recommendations

Case Study 20—CEO and Board of Directors—Prophecy—Things to Come

Topic introduction: Have you published a list of things-to-come actions as part of your plans to alter the future? If not, why not? If not, do you believe you should reconsider and now prepare and publish such a list? If not, why not? If yes, what are they?

Reader Topic Analysis

Reader Conclusions and Recommendations

Case Study 21—CEO and Board of Directors—Prophecy—Serendipity Pools

Topic introduction: Have you ever discussed the concept of serendipity pools in a board meeting? If not, would you? Should you? If not, why not?

Reader Topic Analysis

Reader Conclusions and Recommendations

Case Study 22—CEO and Board of Directors—Prophecy—A Higher Power

Topic introduction: Have you ever discussed the concept of a higher power in a board meeting? If not, would you? Should you? If not, why not?

Reader Topic Analysis

Reader Conclusions and Recommendations

Case Study 23—CEO and Board of Directors—Prophecy—Technologies of the Times

Topic introduction: Have you published a list of the technologies of the times? If not, why not? If yes, what does the list look like?

Reader Topic Analysis

Reader Conclusions and Recommendations

Case Study 24—CEO and Board of Directors—Prophecy—Swings in the Civil Society Pendulum

Topic introduction: Do you analyze and make predictions of swings in the civil society pendulum? If not, why not? If yes, what would such a list of predictions look like?

Reader Topic Analysis

___

Reader Conclusions and Recommendations

___

Case Study 25—CEO and Board of Directors—Prophecy before Vision

Topic introduction: After reading and studying this book, do you now believe it is possible for you to see and predict the future? Do you believe that there are events to happen, as described in this book and nothing can be done to change or prevent them from happening? Do you now believe you can alter the future through the concept of things to come? Do you believe you and your people can always be the smartest in the room? Do you believe you can make the right decision every time with only ten percent of the information? Do you believe there are signs from a higher power to guide you if you act for the good?

For each of these questions, if not, why not? If yes, please explain why. If yes, would you always have said yes?

Reader Topic Analysis

___

Reader Conclusions and Recommendations

CHAPTER 7

MY PROPHECIES FOR THE TWENTY-FIRST CENTURY

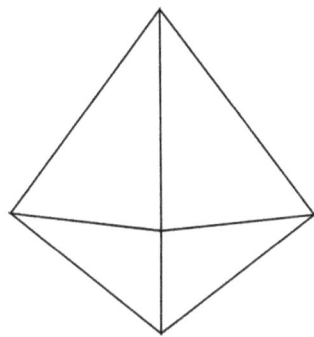

As the last chapter of each book I write, I include my cumulative list of prophecies for the twenty-first century. In chapter 3, I said you must be willing to openly publish your prophecies. If you are not willing to openly publish them, you are not really confident in your prophecies. Besides, what better way to embarrass my grandchildren in the future than to leave them to see how wrong I was.

THE LIST OF JAMES MICHAEL MATTHEW PROPHECIES FOR THE TWENTY-FIRST CENTURY

Prophecy 1: The populations of China and the United States will crisscross at approximately 650 million people.

Prophecy 2: The population of Florida will reach sixty million people, approximating the size of Japan's population and economy at the end of the century.

Prophecy 3: Countries that successfully integrate multicultural, ethnic, racial, and religious populations will dominate their regions of the world.

Prophecy 4: By the year 2090, some form of democracy will be the only form of government existing in the world. All communist and dictatorship forms of political systems will cease to exist.

Prophecy 5: More people in Asia will speak English than not.

Prophecy 6: The countries of the Western Hemisphere will integrate politically, economically, and culturally far more than ever attempted before. These integrations will be enshrined with multiple treaties and agreements never before used.

Prophecy 7: By the year 2050, the Nations of the World will understand the road to defeating ancient climate change runs through the great deserts of the planet.

PROPHECY BEFORE VISION

CHAPTER 8

LET'S PLAY PROPHECY POKER

PROPHECY POKER

As outlined in figure 4 in chapter 3, we believe we have three significant opportunities from three events to happen. Let's have some fun in this chapter and continue the fun for several years. Let's assume each predicted event-to-happen-strategy is a poker table. The game is seven-card draw. There are five players at each table, so I have four opponents at each table. With each new book, I will be asking my readers to let me know where you think I stand, or one year later, whichever comes first. Let's play!

Table 1 - Event To Happen - Coming Collapse of China

- Player - Chinese Investors
- Player - Chinese Allies
- Player - Chinese Supply Chains
- Player - Chinese Communist Party
- Player - JM Prophecies

(Center: Table 1 Coming Collapse of China)

Table 2 - Event To Happen - Coming Consumer Rejection of Contemporary Media & Entertainment Industries

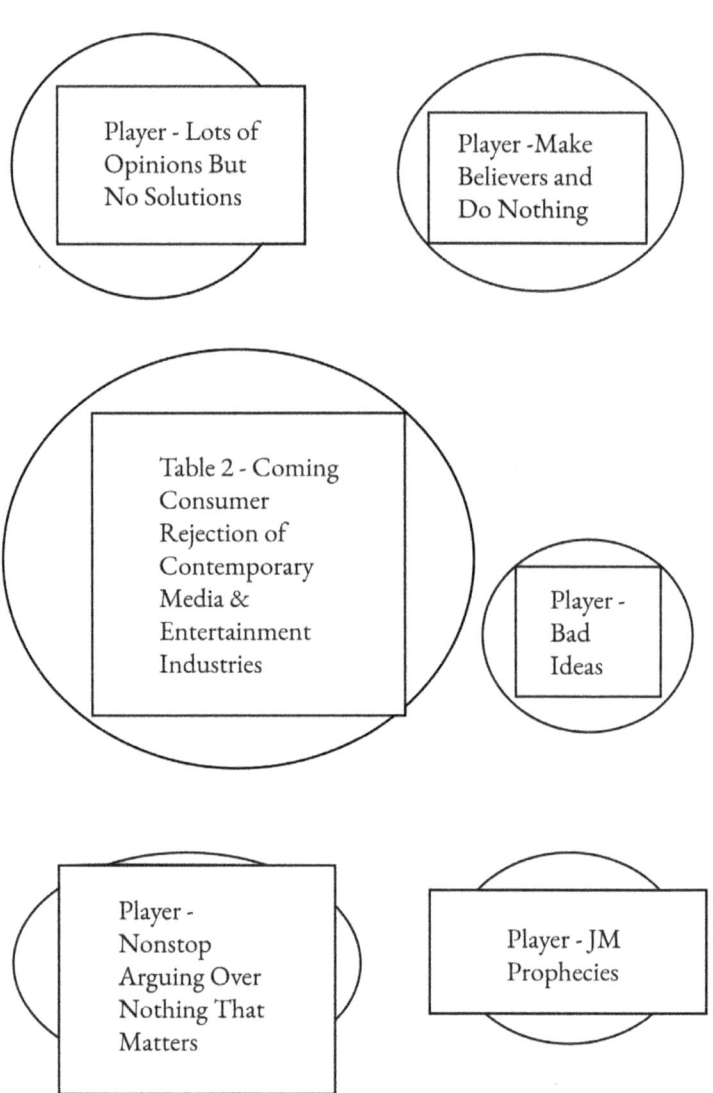

PROPHECY BEFORE VISION

Table 3 - Event To Happen - Coming Combined Tsunami of Aging Population & Wealth Inequality Pyramid

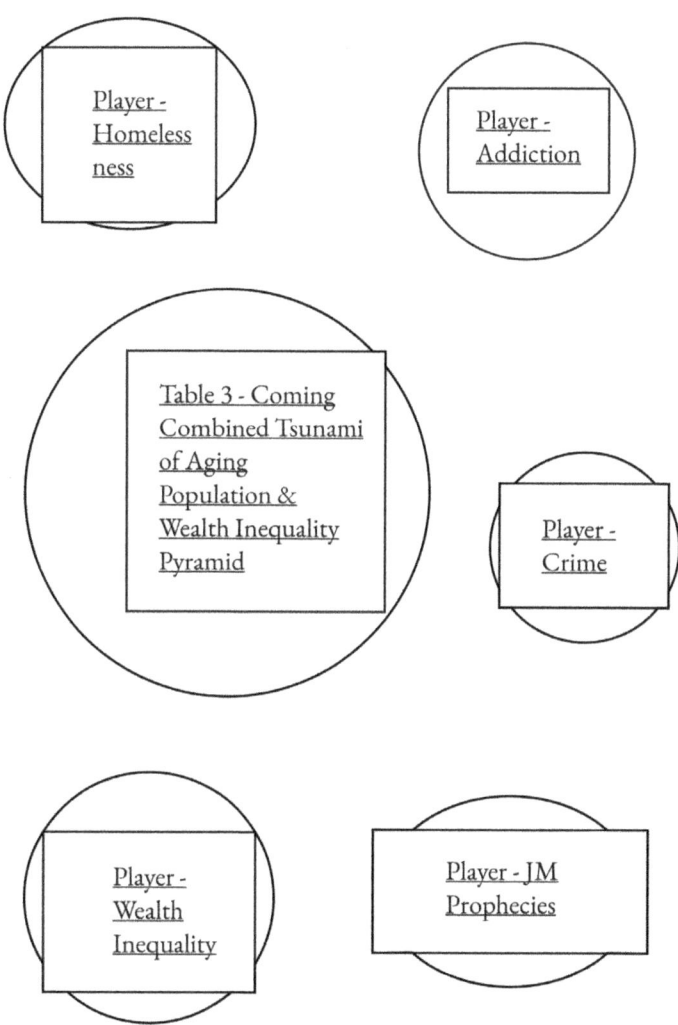

NOTES

Chapter 1

1. "Prophecy before Vision—Learning to See and Alter the Future."
2. The serfdoms of our times.
3. "True power lies in the masses, not for what they own but for what they can produce and consume over their lifetimes."
4. "The JM Prophecies Five Steps to Invert Income and Wealth Inequality Pyramids."
5. To invert the global wealth inequality pyramid, both to change the world and because that is where the big opportunities are.
6. Leadership means helping others be successful.
7. Generosity is the new currency of our times.
8. Target markets begin at the very bottom of the inequality pyramid.
9. "Step 5—Remove Crime, Addiction, Mental Illness, and Homelessness from Communities and Assist Those Populations Separately."
10. JM Prophecies Brain Care.

Chapter 2

1. The three pendulums of a society.
2. The three pendulums exist and operate under the umbrella of global demographics and the umbrella of the technologies of the times.
3. "The Headwaters of Prophecy."
4. "Events to Happen—Things to Come—Learning to See the Future."

5. Global demographics.
6. The technologies of the times.
7. Creation of the intellectual society.
8. Political pendulum under a democratic society.
9. Economic pendulum—capitalistic or not.
10. Civil society pendulum—everything else.
11. Fissures in the three pendulum swings.
12. Positioning yourself on the inside of a pendulum.
13. The power of contrarian thought and strategy for the civil society pendulum.
14. The velocity of pendulum swings.
15. Inequality pyramids for public policy.

Chapter 3

1. "Events to Happen."
2. "Things to Come."
3. Learning to See and altering the future.
4. "The Three Headwaters of Prophecy." These three headwaters are:
    a. global demographics
    b. the technologies of the times
    c. the three pendulums of a society
4. Type I prophecies—global events to happen.
5. Type II prophecies—regional, local, and industry specific events to happen that will impact you and your organization.

6. Establish your serendipity pools.
7. Confronting type II events to happen and channeling things-to-come decisions through your serendipity pool pathways.
8. Power of positioning.
9. JM Prophecies Corporation serendipity pools and things to come pathways example.
10. Embrace your higher power and learn to follow the signs.
11. Decision-making under uncertainty.

Chapter 4

1. Crimes
2. Prisons and prisoners
3. Alcohol and drug addictions
4. Mental illness
5. Homeless
6. Impact on our neighborhoods and civil society
7. Isolation = abuse = bottom of wealth inequality pyramid
8. The financial opportunity for our country
9. The financial opportunity for criminals

Chapter 5

1. The coming economic and social tsunamis of wealth inequality combined with aging populations.

2. It's time to make 180-degree contrarian bets.

3. What is our future transportation infrastructure?

Chapter 6

1. Case studies—setting public policy and learning prophecy.

Chapter 7

1. The list of James Michael Matthew prophecies for the twenty-first century.

Chapter 8

1. Let's play prophecy poker.

REFERENCES

1. Professor Mark. A. Cohen, Vanderbilt University, "New Research Examines the Cost of Crime in the U.S., Estimated to Be $2.6 Trillion in a Single Year," February 5, 2021, retrieved June 16, 2021, https://news.vanderbilt.edu/2021/02/05/new-research-examines-the-cost-of-crime-in-the-u-s-estimated-to-be-2-6-trillion-in-a-single-year/.

2. Wendy Sawyer and Peter Wagner, "Mass Incarceration: The Whole Pie 2020," March 24, 2020, retrieved June 16, 2021, https://www.prisonpolicy.org/reports/pie2020.html.

3. Addiction Center, "Statistics on Addiction in America," retrieved June 16, 2021, https://www.addictioncenter.com/addiction/addiction-statistics/.

4. Morgan Solomon-Maynard, "10 Surprising Mental Health Statistics From 2020, Mental Health First Aid" National Council on Mental Wellbeing, November 5/2020, retrieved June 17, 2021, https://www.mentalhealthfirstaid.org/external/2020/11/10-surprising-mental-health-statistics-from-2020/

5. National Institute of Mental Health, "Mental Health," retrieved June 17, 2021, https://www.nimh.nih.gov/health/statistics/mental-illness

6. CDC Centers for Disease Control and Prevention. "Physician Office Visits and Emergency Office Visits," retrieved June 17, 2021, https://www.cdc.gov/nchs/fastats/mental-health.htm

7. John Hopkins Medicine, "Mental Health Disorder Statistics," retrieved June 17, 2021, https://www.hopkinsmedicine.org/health/wellness-and-prevention/mental-health-disorder-statistics.

8. USDebtClock.Org, "US National Debt Clock," retrieved June 17, 2021, https://www.usdebtclock.org

9. Jim Wu, Bank for International Settlements, "Reuters Graphics," retrieved June 17, 2021, http://fingfx.thomsonreuters.com/gfx/rngs/CHINA-DEBT-HOUSEHOLD/010030H712Q/index.html

10. United States Census Bureau, "National Population Projections, 2017," retrieved June 24, 2021, www.census.gov/programs-surveys/popproj.html. https://www.census.gov/newsroom/stories/senior-citizens-day.html.

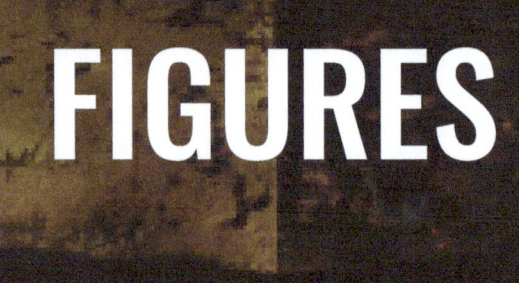

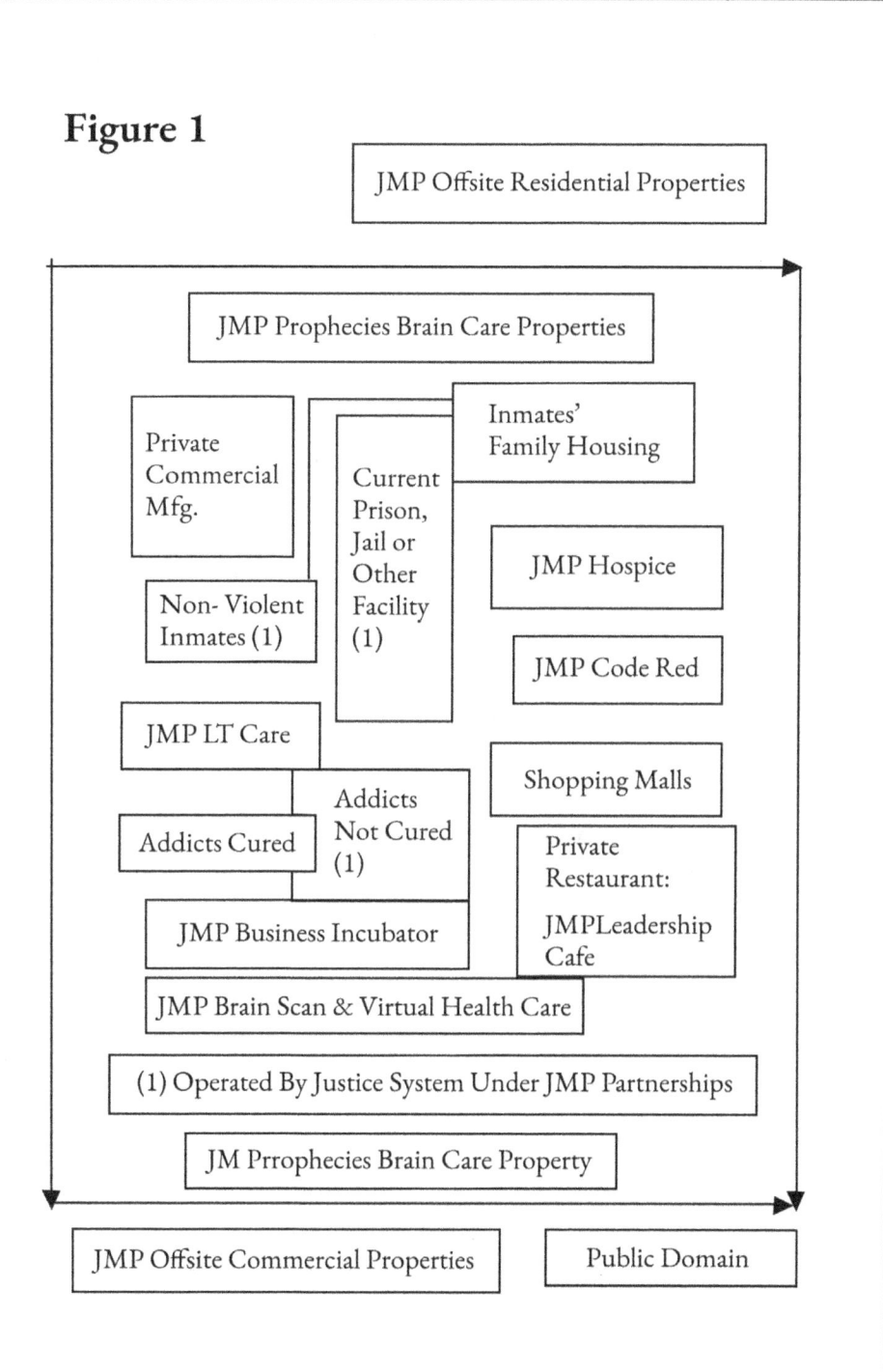

FIGURE 2

**The 3 Pendulums of a Society - They Are Constantly
<u>Swinging Pendulums In Dynamic 3 Dimensions</u>**

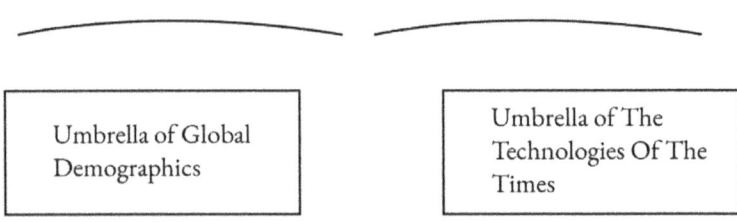

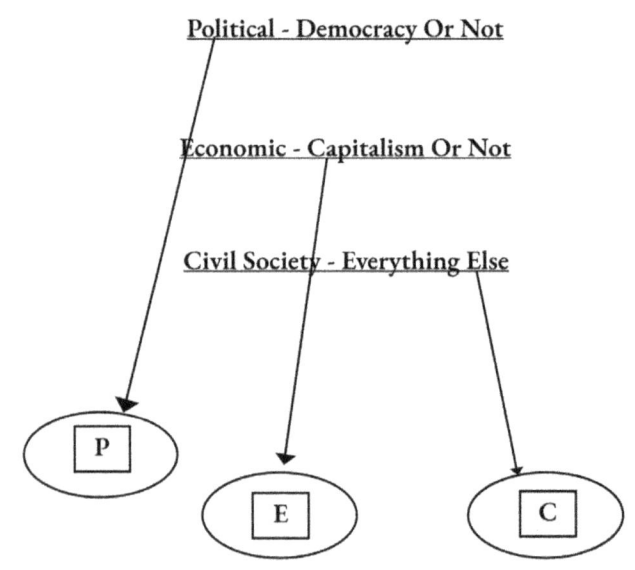

Figure 3
Inequality Pyramids for Public Policy

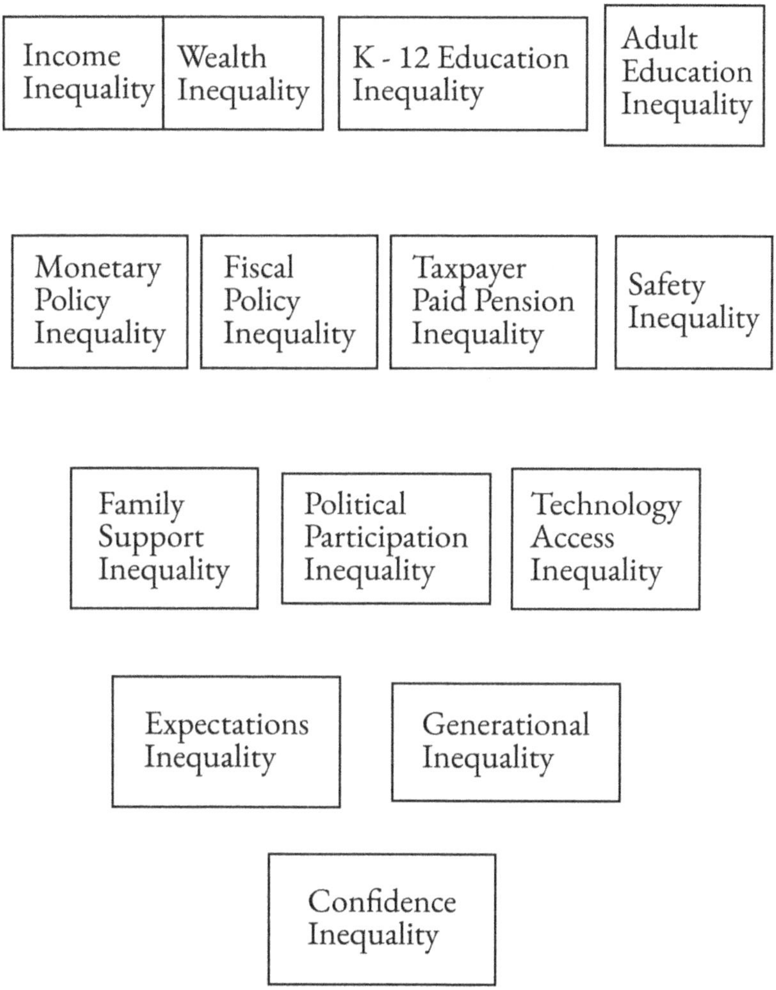

| Income Inequality | Wealth Inequality | K - 12 Education Inequality | Adult Education Inequality |

| Monetary Policy Inequality | Fiscal Policy Inequality | Taxpayer Paid Pension Inequality | Safety Inequality |

| Family Support Inequality | Political Participation Inequality | Technology Access Inequality |

| Expectations Inequality | Generational Inequality |

| Confidence Inequality |

FIGURE 4

JM Prophecies Corporation Serendipity Pools and Pathways for "Things To Come"

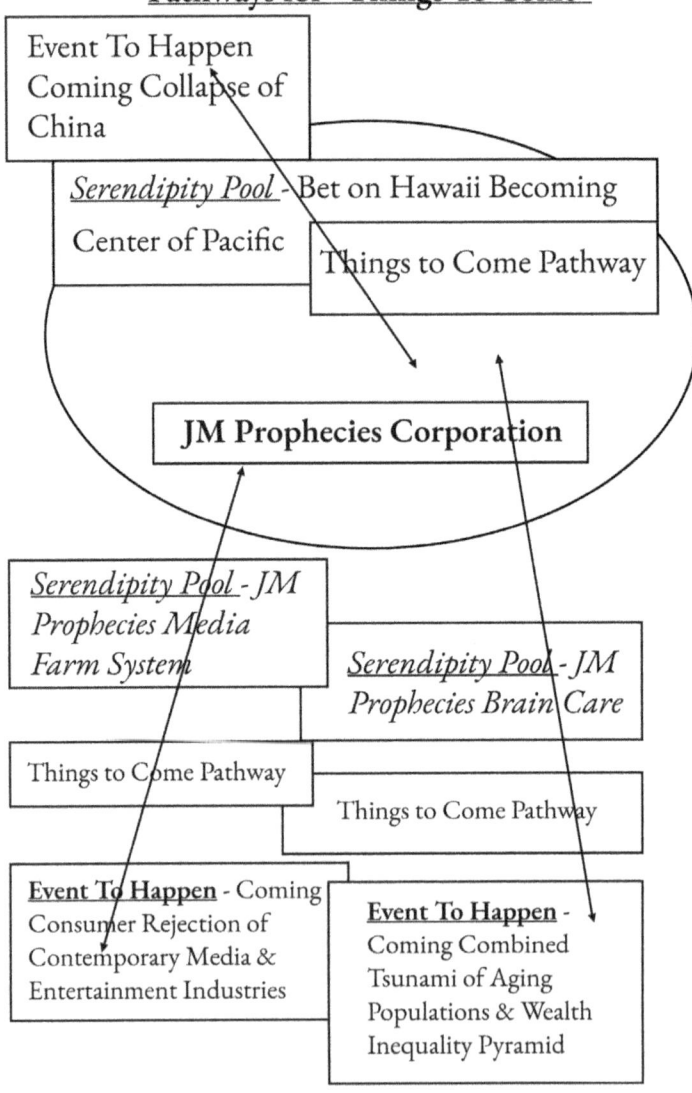

Exibit 1

FROM PYRAMID TO PILLAR

A CENTURY OF CHANGE OF THE UNITED STATES POPULATION

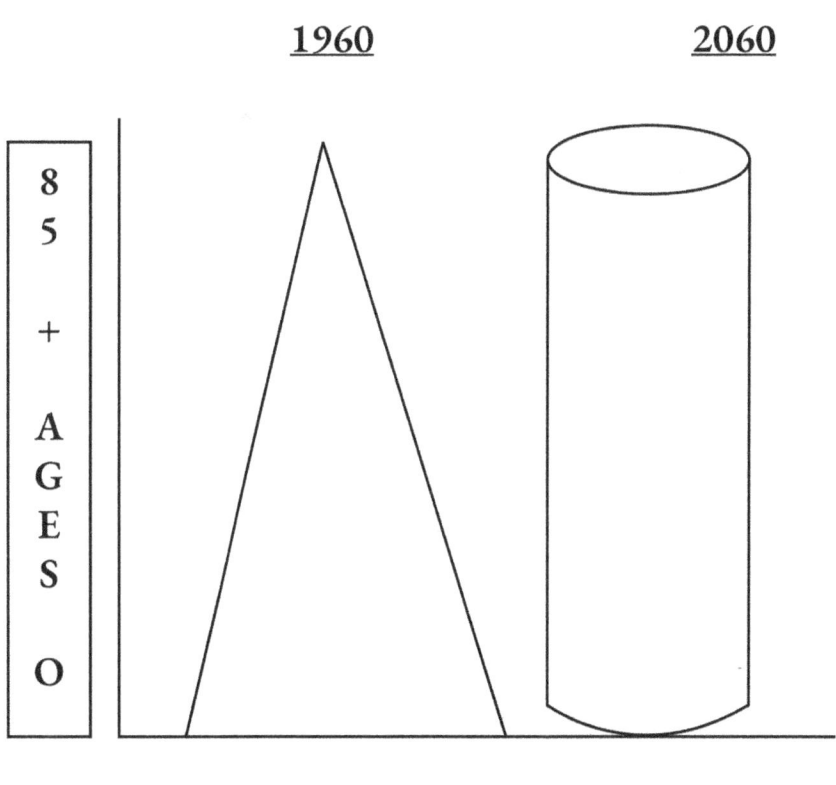

JAMES MICHAEL MATTHEW

PREVIEW

Building Fjords in the Great Deserts – Second Edition

Peer Review

PREVIEW

Manufacture Like Nature Manufactures

Green Chemistry and Biofuels

Understanding Self-Assembly

Reimagining the Periodic Table of Elements

Growing Our Raw Materials

JAMES MICHAEL MATTHEW

PREVIEW

Building Fjords in the Great Deserts – Third Edition

Drafting the Enabling Legislation

PREVIEW

Contrarian Evolution and Contrarian Economics

Saving the Planet and Saving Humanity

JAMES MICHAEL MATTHEW

PREVIEW

5 Million Drone Boats, Ships, and Submersibles

Building a Maritime DNA into American Society

PREVIEW

Preemptive Strike

Events to Happen and Things to Come during World War III

JAMES MICHAEL MATTHEW

PREVIEW

The Next Great Generation

Your Destiny, Your Prophecy, Your Time

www.ingramcontent.com/pod-product-compliance
Lightning Source LLC
Chambersburg PA
CBHW052032030426
42337CB00027B/4974